ROADS
from the
BOTTOM

ROADS
from the
BOTTOM

A Survival Journal for America's Black Community

by

C. K. Chiplin

QUAIL RIDGE PRESS
Brandon, Mississippi

Manufactured in the United States of America

QUAIL RIDGE PRESS
P. O. Box 123 / Brandon, MS 39043
1-800-343-1583

Library of Congress Cataloging-in-Publication Data

Chiplin, C. K. (Charles K.)
  Roads from the Bottom: a survival journal for America's
Black community / by C.K. Chiplin.
        p.   cm.
  ISBN 0-937552-73-9
    1. Afro-Americans—Mississippi—Vicksburg—Social life and
customs. 2. Afro-Americans—Mississippi—Vicksburg—Social
conditions. 3. Marcus Bottom (Vicksburg, Miss.)—Biography.
4. Chiplin, C. K. (Charles K.)—Childhood and youth. 5.
Vicksburg (Miss.)—Biography.   I. Title
F349.V6C45 1996   96-28990
976.2′29—dc20   CIP

DEDICATION AND ANTICIPATION

As James Weldon Johnson through the divine inspiration of the Almighty, invoked a blessing of *keeping* for his people, asking—"God of our weary years, God of our silent tears, Thou who hast by Thy might, led us into the light, *keep* us forever in the path we pray"—I as humbly dedicate and anticipate a blessing of *return* for my people. This book is therefore dedicated to the scores of people throughout this Nation and around the world who travel or will begin to travel the *Roads from the Bottom*, dedicating their lives to God and the uplifting of fallen humanity. So then, my supplication is—..."Thou who hast by Thy might, led us into the light, *return* us to the path (roads), we pray."

Finally, from the inner reaches of my heart, I dedicate this historical summation to Angela Griffin for invaluable typing assistance during the preparation of the manuscript and to Alfred St., (Buddy), Jessie Clyde (deceased), Thomas James, Edward Lee, James Taft, Jr., (Boo), Johnnie Mae, Jessie Lee and the two who insisted that we take the right "roads," our parents—Mr. and Mrs. James Taft Chiplin, Sr.

CKC

CONTENTS

Mrs. Rosa Lee Chiplin, a lady of gentle grace and charm. 1955. Photograph by Johnston Photography.

INTRODUCTION

It has been said that "the white man never forgets an enemy, the Indian never forgets a friend, but the black man forgets everybody." While I take issue with the generalization implied, I am determined that the great efforts and undying love shared by my parents will not be silently closed away only in our memories, then buried as we must depart this life.

Chiplin children to come must grow up in a world that will no doubt shake the very rafters of human existence. Generations of children to come will only endure as we make an effort to share with them the time-tried wisdom that keeps and saves — saves when all the odds are seemingly against you — saves when you show up daily in a hate-filled, prejudiced society, with a black face — saves when other blacks are bent on destroying due to their own miseducation and misfortunes of non-memory and historical non-recall.

Black communities throughout this nation are threatened daily by blatant acts of crime and violence. We are now fearful of our children and for good reasons. While many black adults of recent decades fought for the chance to live and let live, many children of the 1990s are fighting for the chance to die.

How and when did we get ourselves into this present state? How will we - or will we - survive the bullets of consciousless children? Will our educational institutions remain viable as they double as battlegrounds?

Perhaps our disregard to the African adage of many years has contributed to our national crisis —
"It takes a whole village to raise a child."

I suspect that this writing will serve as a bridge, a footpath to lead many who will simply read and understand to a point of safety even in this troubled world. I am sure that reflections of the noble efforts of the past along with active memory of the great legacies of love, faith and endurance

9

exemplified in black communities of the not so distant past are very much to our advantage.

I hope that Americans — black, white, others, young, old, wealthy, poor, will gain a lesson as we recall —

"It's an awful long way to the top of the world, on a <u>rock road</u> that winds all around; it's an awful long way to the top of the world — but short is the fall back to the ground." It is certain that vast strides have been made towards closing the national and international gaps of racial indifference and separation. More certain is the fact that blacks in America have fought for and won more rights and a larger portion of liberty. Many blacks have struggled and advanced on the roads from the bottom, but many now travel roads that lead to death and destruction. It is my hope that you will read, reflect and respect our struggle for human equality and then share this message of hope and determination with this and coming generations, lest they take the wrong roads.

THE PROLOGUE
"Roads From the Bottom"

Remember the roads we walked along, in former times
gone by...
Remember the sweetness of our song, As life's moments
swiftly fly.
Remember me when the morning wakes as the robins
sweetly sing—
Remember me when your leisure take or the noon bells
stately ring.
Remember my face, so much like yours,—my color, my
smile, my hair—
Remember me as you do your chores, or kneel in silent
prayer.
Remember the hours of sweat and tears—our struggles for
the race—
Please don't forget me through the years—give me a
special place.
Souls, they linger, last and live, while bodies must decay—
Remembering is not much to give, when I have gone
away.
Each time you're challenged to move ahead—each time
you must stand tall—
Remember the words that I have said—Remember and
recall.
Yes, remember, the long, long dusty roads, the troubled
roads, the calm—
Roads from the bottom with heavy loads—Where black
feet walked along.

1

Way Back Then

My mother and father grew up in Jefferson County in the general vicinity of Rodney and Fayette, Mississippi.

Daddy had previously been married to Lucille. They divorced and he later married Momma (Rosa Lee Synder), who was eight years younger, and 14 years old at the time.

He knew life and all of the stuff that comes with it. His world was one of racism and reality—racism over which he had no control, reality that confounded and confined him to the "short end of the stick." He saw white boys and girls "living large" with little or nothing to do; white girls and boys on the plantation and neighboring plantations to whom he was completed to address as Mr. and Miss; white boys and girls who, through no slip of the tongue, often addressed him as "*nigger*" or "*boy.*"

Jim (Daddy) was bright (not in color), alert and determined—determined to be something in his life time, determined to help his mother and determined to get an education.

As it turned out, his quest for a formal education was terminated around the sixth grade. He chose to stop school to help out after his stepfather was physically impaired having been thrown from a temperamental mule. They called his stepfather Captain, Captain Chiplin. Daddy was not sure and never was told whether Captain Chiplin was his real father or his stepfather.

LESSONS LEARNED IN THE COUNTRY
"STICKING LIKE GLUE"

With so many "dysfunctional," divided, desperate families in present-day society, it is important and interesting to note what kept families—particularly black families,-rural

13

and city—together in the not so distant American past.

Sociologists insist that "poverty breeds violence." If this had been true of our family and where we grew up, our family would have "fought like cats and dogs" constantly and our community would have been a battleground. But that was not the case; a cohesiveness held the family and the community together—a tie that bound—a fellowship of love. I firmly believe that the early years of my immediate family on plantations in Jefferson County had much to do with the endurance needed to make it in a "deprived" community in Vicksburg.

Much like the plantation experience, depravation in the city existed only in terms of material things for mine and other black families.

"YOU CAME UP SHORT"

Plantation life of the 1940s and '50s at a glance immediately brings to mind economic turmoil—days of sweat and tears and nothing, days of struggling and defeat and nothing; days of untold sorrow and nothing,—nothing but love, joy, peace, long suffering, gentleness, goodness and faith— to be sure, the fruits of the spirit—those things that caused our family and other black families to stick together.

How could a family endure when after the crops had been gathered, a visit to the general store (the white man's store where blacks bought seeds, clothes, household items, etc.) revealed the same doleful report to black sharecroppers— *"You came up short!"*—short in terms of not having produced or picked enough cotton on the "halves" to pay the debt. "You came up short" meant that once more, poor black sharecroppers owed the white man, would not have money to meet other basic needs, would have to charge some more and "get deeper in debt."

There is absolutely no doubt that my father and mother utilized endurance skills they learned from the plantation to make it in the city. We often heard the names Jake Wagoner and Mr. Smith—white men who owned plantations— where Daddy and Momma had once worked.

It is quite certain that my father could out-think and out-

14

smart any two white men on a slow day. His uncanny wit and seasoned wisdom fortified the strength, wisdom and love of Momma. Daddy believed that there was always a way out or in or under or through or—kick it down and keep on walking.

REMEMBER THE MULE

Family legend has it that an indifferent, sullen, lazy, rebellious mule had his day of reckoning with Daddy as he worked on Jake Wagoner's plantation. It was somewhere around the summer of 1937. The mule Mr. Wagoner assigned Daddy had historically decided to stop work when the noon whistle blew. For Daddy, the noon whistle only meant that he was, by then, half as tired as he would be by the end of the day—for the mule it meant stop wherever, do not move, count to ten trillion or something close. Daddy

DRAWING BY MICHAEL ALEXANDER

had only plowed several rows of the massive field. Stopping even for lunch was not an active consideration.

There it goes—the noon whistle—sending a course, doleful sound adrift on the murky hot southern summer's day with mosquitoes and molasses-like sweat.

According to Daddy, "I did everything I knew to make that mule pull after the whistle blew. He wouldn't budge— just stood there like, I guess, the jackass he was. I even tried going up to him, pleading in his ear, explaining that I had to get the rows plowed.... He listened, then closed his eyes as if to tune me out.... Once more, I tried to pull him by the rope. No movement.... I went behind him and pushed against his rear.... Not one step he made.... Then, it came to me.... I went over to the edge of the field and got me some sage brush, tied it together, then tied it under the mule's tail.... Then I lit it.... Took a while for it to get to going good. But when it did! Out across the field that mule went running like a racehorse nearing the finish line.... I never laughed so hard in all my life.... Well, after that, Mr. Wagoner gave me another mule and we left that lazy scoundrel around the house.... He did alright around there.... My Momma could get him to do a few things every now and then."

As if we had not all killed ourselves with laughter, Daddy proceeded to give us the next episode in the mule story. He continued... "One day, Momma brought me some lunch out to the field. She came up riding on a wagon with that lazy mule pulling—very slowly.... Momma got down from the wagon and gave me the bucket with some sugar syrup, biscuits and salt meat. After a few words, she was ready to go—the mule wasn't. She climbed back up on the wagon and shouted, 'git up mule!' He looked around as if he wasn't sure who she was talking to or that he was a mule. I had not told Momma about my earlier encounter with that mule and she had no idea what it took to make him pull. Momma was a frilly, well-dressed, proud black woman who, even during those times, somehow came up with many of the finer things in life. This day was no exception, as she sat there all 'starched and ironed' with costume jewelry she had bought from the candy store man shining and jingling. Once more she shouted 'Git up, mule!' Not wanting my mother to faint off sitting there in the sun and wanting to get on with my work, I repeated the ignition process—sagebrush to tail—fire to sagebrush... I thought I had killed my Momma, for she lay stretched out for dead over in the thickets as the mule who sent her wagon on perhaps the first mule drawn air flight on earth, continued to parts unknown.

In 1945, Daddy and Momma decided they had had enough of plantation (strife) life. Without hesitation or much prior thought, Daddy informed Jake Wagoner that he was planning to move his family to Vicksburg. "It's time for me to try something else, Mr. Wagoner," Daddy recalled as he shared that bit of family history. Mr. Wagoner's response was immediate and sharp, "You try to leave this plantation, Jim, I'll kill you!"

Mr. Wagoner's threat only crystallized Daddy's urgency to leave the plantation. Somewhere near the end of summer, he secretly loaded his things and family on the back of a pickup truck that belonged to another black man on the plantation and left Wagoner's late in the night. The 47 miles from Jefferson County to Vicksburg must have seemed awfully long to Daddy and Momma. Thoughts of Jake Wagoner tracking them down lurked in their minds.

Daddy's memory of Jake Wagoner was impacted by thoughts of brutality of blacks who had worked on his plantation. He had often commanded other whites and blacks to abuse them physically. He had a very hostile attitude towards blacks whom he referred to as "uppity niggers," "niggers who don't know their place."

Daddy knew that "his place" was not on Wagoner's plantation because he certainly could not be controlled and was not going to allow his children to suffer at the hands of a temperamental old plantation owner. He recalled, "I told Rosa to get the children (Johnnie Mae; James, Jr; Alfred, Jr.; Edward Lee; Thomas James and Jesse Clyde) dressed before the sun went down. We would leave out about midnight, a time I was sure Mr. Wagoner was asleep. We got up late that night and did not light the lamp for fear Mr. Wagoner would see the light. We only packed those things that we had to have—our clothes, some food and a few other things. I loaded my shotgun because I knew if that evil man had tried to stop me, I was going to shoot him. The only thing that almost gave us away was those old dogs barking and running behind the truck."

Thankfully, Jake Wagoner had not followed the fleeing Chiplins, and they found a safe haven in Vicksburg. According to Daddy, "I knew we had to stay somewhere and by daybreak, I had found a little shotgun house in Smith Alley. The man said it was for rent, but he really wanted to sell it. I moved my family in that same evening and signed to start buying that house."

The new address was 1405 Smith Alley. Smith Alley was just off Halls Ferry Road, in the heart of Marcus Bottom. It was a dirt passage that led from Halls Ferry Road to Alma Street. Mt. Carmel Church was up the hill to the left after turning from Smith Alley onto Alma Street.

Smith Alley, although badly gutted after each rain, was a good place with six shotgun houses and one building that was used for church services. We were told later that our house site perhaps had been a small cemetery years earlier. We never saw any traces of tombstones or graves, but we scared each other silly with ghost stories many nights.

Emma Elliot lived in the rental house to the left of ours. Miss Emma, a beautician, very lively and spirited, would drink excessively. Momma recalled that during their first spring in Smith Alley, Miss Emma "tied one on." As the house became consumed in flames she heard Miss Emma calling out, "Hey Chip, call the fire department, I'm burning this sonna b—— down!" Miss Emma moved after a while and went on to live a very productive life; gave up the bottle, continued her beauty shop and perfected her God-given ability to play the piano.

The small church building to the right of our house was renovated for another shotgun rental house. Next to the former church was a larger house covered with simulated brown brick paper—Miss Rosa Sander's house. Miss Sanders worked in white people's houses. She had an old

18

Chevrolet parked in a locked garage next to the house. She never drove. I remember her walking to work early in the morning and returning late in the evening with brown paper bags in her arms. For some reason, she always called me "Preacher."

Miss Josie Ennon lived just up from Miss Sanders. Her house, although a basic shotgun format, had an addition to the side. Her yard was well-kept and flowed with fruit trees, particularly big, juicy plum trees that remained our constant source of neighborly temptation. Miss Josie was Momma's good friend and was a very generous single lady.

There were only two houses on the other side of Smith Alley—up at the end near to Alma Street. Miss Louise and her family, relatives of the Lassiters (later to become the first family of Mt. Carmel Church) lived there. Mrs. Lula Pugh, Rev. Lassiter's mother, lived in the last house that faced onto Alma Street. Mother Pugh, as we called her, was stout, strong and caring. A lady of few words, her presence was convicting and assuring. When compelled to speak, her few words were resonant and convicting. She was wonderful! Mother Johnson, a devout member of Mt. Carmel, lived just up from Mrs. Pugh. She had managed to purchase new shinny Chrysler cars regularly and was most willing to accomodate others.

Miss Leona lived in the nice shotgun house at the opposite end of Smith Alley facing Halls Ferry Road. She was a hard-working lady who liked nice things and got them.

"OLD MAN RIVER"

Having escaped Jake Wagoner, Daddy took a job within a few days on the levee of the Mississippi River at Vicksburg. His assignments included carrying large bales and bundles from the banks of the river onto barges and helping to pull massive ropes to bring the barges closer into the banks. Daddy said, "Only Negro men and boys worked out on the river. It was hard, back-breaking work. The salary was pretty good, though—50 cents per day." From a net salary of less than three dollars per week, Daddy made house payments and supported his family.

19

Reflecting on his river experiences, Daddy said, "I understand why the man wrote:

> Colored folks work on the Mississippi; colored folks work while the rich man play. Getting no rest from the dawn to the sunset, getting no rest 'til the judgment day...Pull that barge! Tote that bale; you gits a little drunk and you lands in jail. I gets weary and oh so dreary, I'm tired of living but scared of dying; and old man river, he keeps on rolling along."

After several months, Daddy was hired to work at Vicksburg Paint and Glass Company, then owned by Mr. Al Eggins. He swiftly learned the art of glazing and resilvering mirrors. His salary at the glass company was higher—ten dollars per week.

ANOTHER CHILD IS BORN

Soon after moving to Vicksburg, Momma gave birth to

The Chiplin's family house, 1954

another baby girl—the second of three girls (who lived) born to our parents.

Jessie was born on January 24, 1946 in the shotgun house in Smith Alley. Without the comfort and luxury of a hospital, Jessie was delivered by a midwife, who was only referred to as Miss Jessie. Momma's pregnancy and delivery with Jessie were basically normal and uneventful. The only problem experienced by our parents with the birth of their new baby girl was deciding on a name. Daddy wanted her named after the midwife who delivered her—Jessie. Problem—our third oldest brother had chosen the name Jesse Clyde upon his entry to the U.S. Army. His given name was "J. C." and the military would not accept initials for names. Nevertheless, the new baby girl would be called Jessie as a tribute to the noble, strong-willed midwife who took so much pain in her delivery.

Mississippi River Bridge at Vicksburg, old and new.

I AM BORN

On September 9, 1947, Momma, after only seven months of pregnancy, gave birth to her last child, me. Daddy always said I was the "last button that fell off Gabriel's coat." I never knew what he meant by that but I was glad to be here.

My untimely delivery, unlike the others was life threatening and Dr. Kinnard, a white doctor whose last name was given as my middle name, told Daddy he would have to make a decision whether to save his wife or the baby. Daddy told him to save both of them. Thanks.

Unlike Momma's other deliveries by midwives, I was born at Dr. Kinnard's office. Daddy said that Momma had been so sick while carrying me that he would not risk the services of a midwife at the house.

2

Mt. Israel Church

BACK DOWN HOME

Although Momma and Daddy had immediately joined Mt. Carmel Church in Vicksburg, their deep spiritual ties with the "home church," Mt. Israel, back down in Jefferson County, continued. Mt. Israel met on the second Sunday of each month, Mt. Carmel met on the first Sunday, thus facilitating our visits "back home."

Early each second Sunday morning, we excitedly prepared for the 47-mile ride to Jefferson County. Daddy used a truck from the glass company for our transportation.

Mt. Israel Church was pastored by Rev. L. L. Miller, a forceful and articulate man. By profession, he was a barber, and I recall how clean cut and neat he always appeared. People looked up to Rev. Miller and were often spell-bound under the throes of his rich, melodic gospel-enriched voice.

Winter meant a cold building inadequately heated by two old iron wood heaters, and summer meant fanning with cardboard fans supplied by the funeral home, but these hardships had no obvious bearing on the long services.

We generally arrived at the church around 10:30. By this time, the building was filled with people who wore their Sunday finest—we used to call it "Sunday go to meeting clothes." Members of the Mothers' Board wore the whitest starch and ironed dresses, as did ladies on the Ushers' Board. Hats for the "women of fashion" were an array of floral depictions ranging from roses to sunflowers. The men's neckties were so wide that I always feared for their safety as the "noose" tied at the tops seemed to make them uncomfortable almost to the point of choking. In high moments, nearing the end of his sermons, Rev. Miller always loosened his necktie and fanned with a white handkerchief—even in the winter. There was something very meaningful about the sound of feet stomping on the wood planked floors of that old wooden building—perhaps notions of a tribal extension. Black folks in the country could not afford stained glass windows, so they painted the glass usually with red, yellow and blue paint. An old rustic water bucket and dipper at the front entrance of Mt. Israel served to quench the thirst of loyal worshippers, many of whom had walked for miles to church. There was an old upright piano with missing keys that didn't seem to bother the lady who only played a select few anyway. Nonetheless the unrehearsed choir bellowed —

"T'will be glory, wondrous glory when we reach that other shore (that other shore); T'will be glory, wondrous glory, praising Jesus ever more!"

Singing was sporadic and traceable to the African notion of "call and response." In a far corner of the church, a deacon would rise and sing—'Before this time another year..." The congregation responded—"B-E-F-O-R-E, T-H-I-S, T-I-M-E, A-N-O-T-H-E-R, Y-E-A-R. Then the deacon, about to shout blurted, "I may be dead and gone!" The audience responded by repeating his phrase and he went on to lead them in others—"I know I am a child of God, although I move so slow;" "I'm bound to meet the court above, and pay for all I've done," etc.

The close of the three-and-a-half hour service meant we would finally go back up to Fayette, Mississippi and eat dinner at Ma Lucy's house (Momma's mother). Ma Lucy was a strong-willed, part-white, part-Indian, black woman. Her house—a shotgun house over in "the quarters"—was spotless clean all the time. In fact, she even swept the grassless ground outside the house.

First Sunday dinner at Ma Lucy's house was as a country reunion once per month where present was the all-enveloping smell of baked chicken, fried chicken, beef and pork roast, field peas, dressing, okra, and always Ma Lucy's famous pound cake. With a little luck, dinner was topped off with homemade vanilla ice cream. The small children always wanted to turn the crank on the wooden ice cream freezer. We turned and turned until the ice cream was almost made, then the older, stronger folks finished the job off.

Ma Lucy referred to Daddy as "son," denoting her deep love and affection for him. He was smart and she knew it. Certainly any man who exchanged marriage vows with my mother had to be smart.

Momma had a sister, Johnnie Mae Starks, and a brother, Edward Synder. (Both are still living in Fayette, Mississippi.) "Aunt Shug," Momma's sister was a very intelligent woman. She completed eighth grade in Fayette and moved to Vicksburg, where she lived with Momma and Daddy to complete high school. (Many rural towns in the South during the 1940s and '50s did not provide public school education for blacks beyond the eighth and rarely the tenth grade.)

Momma's brother, Edward Synder, was in the Army. A tall man of stature, he was a hard worker.

There was a deep bond between Momma, her brother and sister. The three respected their mother and were there for her every beck and call.

As the first Sunday waxed to an end, we prepared to leave for home—back home to Vicksburg—Marcus Bottom. Leaving was never without scores of bundles and wrapped packages of food enough to last several days thereafter.

3

Experiences in the Country

Jessie and I spent our summers in Fayette, Mississippi. We looked forward to the end of school years 1954 through 1960. Somewhere around the first of June we packed for our two-month stay with Momma Lucy (our mother's grandmother) and Aunt Shug (Momma's sister). Life was slow and fun.

For many years Momma Lucy lived across the road from Aunt Shug in The Quarters—a Black settlement of mostly shotgun houses. Typically, the walls of the houses were skillfully papered with newspaper. Glass windows were not very prevalent during that time and many houses, including Momma Lucy's, had wooden shutters that were opened in the summer to let in fresh air and mosquitoes. Water was supplied from a hydrant in a yard just down from Momma Lucy's. One of our daily chores was to walk down the gravel road and fill the water buckets with water for multiple purposes.

The "restroom" (outhouse) was located behind the house. Most of the time we used the "slop pot" inside to avoid going to the outhouse. Have you ever been to an outhouse? Perhaps not. Envision a little wooden hut approximately five feet by five feet; no light; dirt floor; wooden stool constructed above a small well of water with a stench to be avoided even by buzzards; no mirror on the wall—how could you see yourself anyway? no toilet tissue rack—because other sanitary aids were used—corn shucks, newspaper, sorted and crinkled paper bag pieces. I recall that my mother's brother, Uncle Edward, was bitten by a black widow spider as he sat on the stool in the outhouse. Near death, he was tested and treated twenty miles away at a hospital in Natchez, Mississippi. I recall that Miss Mutt, a neighbor down the road from Momma Lucy's alarmed the neighborhood as she fled her outhouse early in the morning, frantically pulling up her under clothes, having seen a rattlesnake during her trip to the outhouse. That's why we used the slop pot.

No one ever explained why people, particularly Momma Lucy, insisted on sweeping the yard. We were instructed to sweep the dust off the dirt (there was little grass). Why did they want "clean dirt?" For whatever reasons, daily we made sure that the yard was clean. But, not only the yard, Momma Lucy crawled under the house and swept—strange? Maybe not. She often reminded us that "cleanliness was next to godliness." The few chickens that roamed about the yard had no regard for Momma Lucy's theology and throughout the day we swept up droppings.

It still amazes me how soft and comfortable the mattresses on her beds were, although they were stuffed with corn shucks. I remember her stirring the shucks in the mattress to even them out. She even went to the trouble of ironing the sheets and pillowcases after lightly starching them. By the way, the pillowcases and sheets were often most times made from bleached flour sacks. I also never figured out the miracle of blueing—a blue sort of additive that turned Momma Lucy's washwater dark blue, but made the clothes sparkling white. Sometimes she would make us pull off our shoes (the few times we had any on) and "tromp" the clothes in the wash tub with our feet. How she was able to hold three clothespins tightly with her lips while smoking a cigarette as she hung out clothes on the "50-mile long" clothesline still confuses me. One day while running through the yard, Teeny (my first cousin, Claudine Starks Middleton) and I knocked the prop from under the clothes line, dropping her prize winning wash on the recenty rain-soaked ground. She overtook us on foot, popping us with a wet towel as we tried to explain that her dog, Skipper, had done it. "You must tell a lie and the truth ain't in you!" she yelled as Skipper, securely chained, jumped up and down and barked at us for lying on him. Never did like that dog.

Momma Lucy was a hard working, strong willed woman. She was employed for many years as the maid and cook in

27

Mr. Fred Youngblood's house. She spoke often of Mr. and Mrs. Youngblood and how nice they were to her. No one ever mentioned how nice she was to them—showing up six days a week, thoroughly cleaning their house, putting out garbage, and of course preparing the daily meals and leaving Sunday dinner prepared for them to heat up—all for the grand total of nine dollars per week. Even then, nine dollars could not adequately sustain Momma Lucy. What did sustain her were her great faith and unusual management abilities. She had a ticket account at a grocery store up town. It was always paid in full and on time.

Although it was in the quarters, Momma Lucy's house literally glowed as did her employers'. She was pleased to receive secondhand things and make them look brandnew. Newer still was her daily determination as she strutted with pride to and from the white folks' house.

Although her formal education was limited, she listened well and learned many lessons. Her vocabulary was remarkable and we often laughed when she used words in conversation that we thought she had made up, such as "all she was saying was defamation;" "he was driving and veered to the side;" "you shan't have it!" *Webster's New World Dictionary* defines defamation as words spoken that injures a person's reputation; veer—to change sides; and shan't as a contraction for shall not.

The first time I heard Momma Lucy use "shan't" was as she chased her dog Skipper, who for some reason had mustered up enough nerve to run through the front door of her shotgun house and swiftly retrieve a bone that she had just dropped from a tin pan. Skipper ran a marathon pace through the back door and at least five rounds around the outside with Momma Lucy in hot pursuit shouting, "You shan't have it." He didn't! Hot, angry and exhausted, Momma Lucy threw the bone with all her might into the distance out back and rechained Skipper. The neighbors' dogs competitively pulled at the meaty hambone as Skipper drooled.

Momma Lucy used other words that were common in the country such as: fit (defined as an outburst of anger or fight); fork—(a turn off the road); yesditty—(yesterday); garry—

"Momma Lucy" - Lucy Kelly Johnson

(porch); peer (look); doso (couch); and jek (precook vegetables for freezing or canning). Several of her words were home-spun. For instance, miration (admiration) and traping (walking in and out of a house), and most often used as she yelled at us after moping the floor.

Additionally, Momma Lucy was a human adding machine and calculator, able to add long lists of numbers, multiply large numbers and do long division mentally while we desperately figured on paper.

A woman of mixed racial background—Indian, white and black, she was of stately build with long black straight hair, and she looked almost white in appearance. Her rare beauty had earlier caught the attention of a Jefferson County plantation owner, who wanted to marry her. Of his romantic advances she said, "I could have married him and been the envy of a lot of ladies—Black and white—but his money could not buy me. He wanted to leave his wife and I didn't want any part of that! I knew that if I just trusted in the good Lord things would get better."

Once Momma Lucy lowered her guard and allowed the regular visitation of a male friend called Buddy Man. She was extremely kind to him, but in return he was extremely rude and abusive. One summer's night about 11:30, Buddy Man knocked loudly at the front door. He had been drinking and wanted Momma Lucy to cook for him. "Buddy Man, I told you not to come by here this time of the night! We trying to get some sleep!", she told him as he stood just inside the front door. He slapped her. I remember her night gown flying through the air as she ran to the kitchen shouting, "What do you want—hoe cakes, hot cakes or flitidabs (a kind of skillet cornbread)." Not many weeks thereafter, Buddy Man blackened her eye. That certainly was the final straw as my mother and her sister, Aunt Shug, intervened. Most women in the country were strong. Too strong to allow their men or anybody else to abuse them. Unfortunately, Momma Lucy had gained in years and was less likely to defend herself. Buddy Man was forbidden to ever come near her again. He didn't. Even of that experience, Momma Lucy remarked, "I know he was wrong, but God's got a watchful

30

eye and things are going to get better!" She believed in "better."

To some extent things did "get better" much later on in Fayette, Mississippi. The Civil Rights movement hit there in full scale around 1965. Charles Evers, then Field Secretary for the NAACP, began voter registration and freedom rallies. Momma Lucy, Uncle Red and Aunt Shug "went out to the meeting" and were supportive of Evers' successful bid for mayor, thereby changing the course of history for Jefferson County.

"Momma Lucy" and Aunt "Shug" (Johnnie Mae Starks) share a Christmas in Marcus Bottom, 1964.

4

Will The Real "Daddy" Please Stand Up!

For well over 80 years, the question of who my Daddy's Daddy really was has not been answered. Daddy bore Captain Chiplin's last name, but when confronted with the question—"Was he Daddy's real Daddy?"—Auntie (my grandmother) would give a quick laugh and tell us to mind our own business. We were certain that if Captain had been Daddy's biological father, she would have been delighted to tell us.

To add to our and Daddy's confusion, there was a man in Auntie's life, a Mr. Eddie Gray who hailed from Mound, Louisiana, just across the bridge from Vicksburg. Mr. Gray, who had known Auntie for some time before Daddy's birth, was the "spitting" image of my father, an absolute copy, voice and all. One day, as a child, I remember looking closely at him as he sat on our front porch in Smith Alley, Vicksburg, Mississippi. The sunlight struck him in such a way that accented his features. There was no doubt that he was my granddaddy. (I guess.)

Even more interesting and perhaps convincing is the fact that Mr. Gray's other son, Andrew Gray, (Daddy's brother from Cleveland, Ohio), had a striking resemblance to my father. They shared as brothers do—holiday visits, trips back and forth from Cleveland, Ohio to Vicksburg.

We finally resolved to leave the matter unresolved and appreciate having at least had two strong black men to claim or disclaim as a grandfather.

5

Daily Life In Marcus Bottom

As a child growing up in "the bottom" around the years 1951 to 1960, it seemed that everything there was so big and the roads that led from there so long. The white folks' houses at the top of the hills seemed so far away, so beautiful, and...so separated from us.

There was a rich sense of pride in the Bottom. People worked hard for what little they had and were more than willing to share. Our next door neighbors, Mr. and Mrs. Gibson (Maggie and Johnnie), always had a nice Chevrolet. Whenever they went to town or the "big grocery store" (supermarkets—Piggly Wiggly or Humpty Dumpty), they offered my parents a ride or would bring back packages for them when my father did not have use of the company truck or before he bought his first truck.

Some other blacks in the community had cars that seemed to shine like new money. They drove them proudly and just as proudly offered transportation to their neighbors.

A WALK THROUGH THE BACK ALLEY

On a typical summer's evening, a walk up the Back Alley led you past friends and neighbors who religiously sat out on their front porches. With a good day's work done and dinner behind them, the back alley folks fraternized from front porch to front porch.

Miss Gistina and Mr. Joe's house was first on the left. I am certain that Jackie "Moms" Mabley borrowed her material from Miss Gistina. She had (and still has) a way of sitting back in her legs, looking you squarely in the eye and relieving whatever frustrations by saying "Boy, I will beat the laying down hell out of you!" Then came her big grin and gutty laugh as she proceeded with a joke. "There was this little old guy who went into a bar and sat on a high stool. This other big guy came in, knocked him off the stool and left saying, 'When that fool comes to, tell him that was Judo!' The very next night—little guy sat on the stool—big guy returned, knocked him off and left saying, 'When he comes to, tell him that was karate.' Came the third night, the big guy repeated his attack on the little guy and left the message, 'Tell him that was Kung Fu!" The very next night, the little guy arrived later at the bar. The big guy sat at the bar. Little guy eased up behind him, knocked him off the stool and strutted proudly to the door proclaiming, 'When that fool wakes up, tell him that was Sears Roebuck hammer!'"

Mr. Joe, Miss Gistina's husband, was a mechanic. He was a good complement to her, as he was generally subdued and let her do most of the talking. Their two children, Betty and Junior, were among our closest friends and were along the same age. Betty was just as witty as her mother and Junior was laid back like his father.

Just up the alley was Miss Magg (short for Maggie). Courteous, kind—and starched and ironed. Even sitting out on the front porch was occasion enough for her to dress up— well, in comparison to others whose front porch sitting clothes ranged from bare backs (men only) to dusters and housecoats for women.

A further stroll on the sulky, mosquito-biting, lightning bug lighting (by the way, what ever happened to the lightning bug?— haven't seen one since back then), Marcus Bottom kind of night carried you to the Queens' house—Miss Zola, Joy, Ruby, Ronald and Rita. They just don't make folks like that anymore. Their family bond was intense. They were good people who cared about everybody, looked out for everybody, particularly their next door neighbors and relatives—the Wooleys—William Wooley, his wife Miss Bessie and their children—Brenda, Bonita and Billy (William, Jr.) Later, they had another girl, Tammy. Miss Sevilla Burnes (Momma Kooney), lived in the house almost facing the Black Alley on Lummie Street along with her sister, Miss Baby. Momma Kooney was a strong member of Mt. Carmel

34

A glance at the "Back Alley"—Marcus Bottom.

In each direction leaving the Bottom, whites lived in mansions like this.

Church and commanded the love, trust and respect of the community. Miss Baby was a member of the Ushers' Board and could be counted on for her close adherence to church rules—no talking during service and chew gum under the threat of losing your life.

Coming back down on the other side of the Back Alley were other shotgun houses (rent houses) where Francis (Miss Gistina's sister), her husband, John, and children—Dotty and Little Jr. lived, not too far up from Johnny Carey's house—previously mentioned.

Just before the Careys' was Miss Sarah Barnes (not related to Miss Baby). Miss Sarah was a bit stern and kept an unnervingly watchful eye over us children. Her smiles were rare and at first, I was scared of her. I later found out that not only could she smile, but she could laugh—loudly and for long periods of time.

Miss Gistina's mother, Miss Luela Harding, lived across the Alley from her. We liked her. After all, she had a big pear tree in the yard and shared freely—after they were ripe. How were children who slipped over fences supposed to know that green pears and plums would make you sick and get you a whipping?

Miss Luela took in ironing from the white folks. I vividly remember shiny Plymouths and Dodges stopping in front of her house, horns blowing and wash baskets being taken from back seats. Even before she got an electric iron, Miss Luela skillfully and artistically washed and ironed her patrons' clothes. She used bluing. Why did white clothes come out heavenly white from a wash in deep blue water? —I never knew. Elijah (Lajah), Miss Luela's son lived with her. He was most mannerable—a tall man who associated with the men who hung out under the tree and other people. Miss Luela had a special way of calling out his name—in fact she could call him from one end of the Alley to the far end....

OTHER NEIGHBORS

Mr. and Mrs. Roosevelt Washington lived in a comparatively nice house around on Halls Ferry Road. Mrs. Washington (Rosa Washington) became Momma's best friend and her husband (Mr. Red) and Daddy were baseball buddies. Mr. Red was deliberate of speech, wise and caring, willing at all times to share anything he had with neighbors. He worked for many years at Anderson Tully, a sawmill up Highway 61 North.

After driving Momma and Daddy to the grocery store on Saturdays, Mr. Red came over and listened to Dizzy Dean, the baseball radio announcer. Momma and Mrs. Rosa sat from house to house as their husbands were totally occupied, glued to the radio. They knew the batting averages of anybody who ever played National League Baseball, loved Dizzy Dean and sang with the theme song: *"Take me out to the ball game, take me out to the crowd, buy me some peanuts and crackerjacks, I don't care if we never come back; so we'll root, root, root for the home team, if we don't win it's a shame, And it's one, two, three strikes you're out at the old ball game!"*

Mr. Red and Daddy rooted even harder for their families and were determined that they would not be "struck out" in life's game. They shared evening and late night porch visits talking about the Bible, their children, their community and their problems. As Momma and Mrs. Washington became sisters, Daddy and Mr. Red became brothers. Mrs. Rosa Washington was Jessie's godmother. Her next door neighbor, Mrs. Lucille Moore, claimed me for her godson and her husband, Mr. Carter Moore, was always very kind to me.

Momma and Daddy made friends with the Burnhams— Mr. and Mrs. Burnham and their children, Jimmy, Baby Sister, Linda and Allen Wayne, who lived not too far from the Bottom on Jeanette Street. Their neighbors, Rev. and Mrs. E. S. Hicks and their children, Rose and Velma, became our friends. Many evenings we would walk from Smith's Alley over to Roosevelt Street to visit with the Burnhams and Hicks.

THE GAMES PEOPLE PLAYED—
THE TOYS THEY PLAYED WITH

"Last night, night before, 24 robbers at my door, I got up, let them in—hit them in the head with a rolling pin!—All hid?!," the counter at the base with back turned and eyes closed called out. This was repeated several times and often the counter had to use additional rhymes if all the children were not hidden... "One box of washing powder, two bars of soap, all who ain't hid holler—billy goat!" If no one cried "billy goat," the counter set out to find the hidden children who tried to out run him/her back to the base to "get their hundred" and not be put out. Those who had either gotten their hundred (touched the base before the counter) or been put out, stood around warning those who remained hidden to watch out for the approaching counter. They cried, "Lay low chicken, with your head cut off!" We were children, with childish hearts and innocent spirits. How were we supposed to understand grownup stuff like— if you have 24 robbers at your door, and you get up and let them in chances are slim to none that you will manage to hit all of them in the head with a rolling pin. We never considered the fact that a chicken with his head cut off had no other option but to "lay low." We lived in worlds of fantasy and make-believe. It was wonderful!

We learned that cooperative efforts work, as everybody pitched in to make wooden wagons, repair old bicycles, and build playhouses (usually under the houses that were very high off the ground). It didn't matter that limited toy purchases were reserved for Christmas when most of us pretended to believe in Santa Claus. Daddy played Santa Claus for us until we were around six or seven, then he explained that Christmas was the celebration of the birth of Christ. It took some getting used to, but he also said, "There really is a Santa Claus—me." He wanted us to value giving and receiving gifts and did not want us to think that a white man had miraculously come down our chimney on Christmas Eve.

Christmas in the Bottom lasted all year because we kept making brand new toys that didn't cost our parents one cent—sling shots, rubber band guns, and pop bottle rings for our fingers. We "motorized" our bicycles with water filled balloons tied against the spokes of bicycle wheels; made hopscotch designs in the dirt; played rock teacher, allowing the players to choose the closed hand they thought the rock was in and advance to the next step higher (grade) by choosing the correct hand; the girls made paper dolls and had dinner parties and always served the child-famous mud cakes. They even managed to swipe enough sugar from the kitchen to sweeten them, making them much more appetizing. We shot marbles, played jacks and ball, cowboys and Indians, and on and on.

We never had a chance to get bored, for there was always so much for us to make up to do. Some of the childhood games were not endorsed by our parents—playing house when little boys and girls assumed what they felt the parents' roles were—you know—hugging and kissing, all that.

Many of us liked to pretend to be cars. We would "Crank up—Whooom! Whooom! Whoom!—and drive off. We always hit on brakes hard once we reached our destination, skidding and making this hideous screech with our mouths. I was always a Chrysler like the one Mrs. Johnson who lived up on Alma Street had.

6

Paying the Cost to be the Boss
(WHO HEADS THE HOUSEHOLD)

Daddy was the respected head of the Chiplin household. He merited this position not only as the major income provider of the family, but because of his assumption of the many related responsibilities. The position of household head did not mean household dictator. He and Momma discussed issues and shared in decisionmaking. They would not allow us to pit one against the other. His answer "no" meant no, and we knew better than to petition to Momma for a different answer. Her response was, "What did your father tell you?"

Heading the household meant leading the household. Daddy led us to Sunday School and church, led family prayer and singing, led us to school functions, and led in completing homework assigned by our teachers. (Yes, there really was a time when students did homework.) We were not to leave our books at school. Momma and Daddy insisted that we needed to study even if the teachers made no home assignments.

White salesmen and insurance collectors learned early not to knock on our door and ask, "Is your mother home?," as they did throughout the black community. We were instructed to tell them, "Yes, but you have to see my father." Daddy told us that "Black men in America have been disrespected as slaves and are still disrespected as free men." He told many stories of how male slaves were beaten and their women used for the sexual gratification of the white man. Moreover, he pointed out that many black women in America had held onto slavery's mental conditioning against their mates and refused to give them the respect they deserved.

Mr. Carmel Church

CHURCH IN THE BOTTOM

Mt. Carmel and King David were the only two Baptist Churches in Marcus Bottom for quite a while. There was a sanctified church near to the bottom just over the hill at the end of Military Street. Sanctified, Baptist, or not yet decided, most people in the Bottom attended church regularly—on their "meeting Sunday." Daddy explained that the concept of "meeting Sunday" for church in the black Community grew out of slavery. Accordingly, four white plantation owners would hire one white preacher to preach to their slaves. Their sermons were always based on one passage of Scripture: "Servants, be obedient to your masters." With four plantations in his charge, the preacher conducted service at one of them each Sunday of the month. Many black churches in the 1950s still held the slavery concept and members of their congregations felt they had fulfilled their Christian responsibility having attended the once

41

per month meeting Sunday.

Mt. Carmel met on the First Sunday each month and the grayish stone building was always filled with people. I could not detect much difference between our services and services back down at Mt. Israel. People shouted just as hard, sang as loudly and prayed as long as they did in the country. There was one slight difference however; people at Mt. Carmel, city people, made an effort to be a bit more proper. Many of them were formerly from the country although some would not admit to it.

Rev. C. C. Claiborne was the church's first pastor that I was old enough to remember. He had been preceded by Reverends Black and Thornton. The pianist was Mrs. Dorothy Shorts. It seemed impossible for anybody's fingers to move as swiftly as hers across the keys as the spirited choir sang... "Tell the angels, tell the angels to make more room; tell the angels, tell the angels, I'll be there soon"..."I am bound for Canaan's land, to that happy golden strand; where I shall receive a blessing for the work I've done below"..."All night, all day, the angels keep watch over me, my Lord; all night, all day, the angels keep watch over me." Rev. Claiborne, in like manner to Rev. Miller back at Mt. Israel, delivered his monthly sermon with much emotion and often ended by singing..."I am tired and weary, but I must toil on until the Lord comes and calls me away; where the morning is bright and the Lamb is the light, and the night is fair as the day...there will be peace in the valley for me, someday, there will be peace in the valley, I pray...."

Rev. Claiborne resigned as pastor of Mt. Carmel and was succeeded by Rev. Wright L. Lassiter, a young man with a large family. Daddy urged the congregation to give him a chance as pastor and felt the church would make much progress under his leadership. It did. Within a few years extensive renovations and additions were completed on the church.

The Lassiter family was highly respected in Vicksburg. Rev. Lassiter made a good living as a brick mason and invested much in his children, all of whom were multi-talented.

(A DISCUSSION OF MUSIC)

Sitting out on the front porch one first Sunday evening in 1955, Daddy talked to us about music in the black church. "People in colored churches always sing about leaving here—going home to glory; the preachers preach about going home to glory. All that's good. I want to go to Glory too, but not right now. I think we should sing about the goodness of God and how He helps us face up to these everyday problems down here. I heard them singing on the radio this morning—'I'm coming up Lord, I'm coming up soon; I'm coming up Lord, I got to hear my doom.' First of all, I'm not coming up, not right now and when I get there, I certainly don't want to hear no doom!" Daddy said as he looked up at the sky as if talking to the people up there. He continued, "There are so many songs that can uplift the spirit, some of them are old songs like Amazing Grace. The man who wrote that song was a mean slave trader who was sailing to America with a ship load of Negro slaves. He cussed all the time. One day one of his slave cooks got up enough nerve and told him he ought to cut that cussing out. He beat her. A violent storm arose at sea that night. He fell down on his knees and prayed for the first time in his life—Lord, save my ship, save my slaves and save me. They were all saved. When he finally reached America, he set his slaves free, took his pen and wrote—"Amazing Grace, how sweet the sound, that saved a wretch like me; I once was lost, but now I'm found, was blind, but now I see...Through many dangers, toils and snares, I have already come, t'was grace that brought me safe thus far and grace will lead me on."

When he finished his stories about music in the church, he said that he wanted Jessie Lee and Johnnie to start taking music from Mr. Harry Clay. The arrangements were made and the lessons were started. He and Momma were proud of their daughters going off one evening per week to music, hoping that they would one day be able to play at the church. Johnnie Mae took her fifty cent music lesson money, skipped the music lessons and bought pickles. Jessie was very serious and advanced through the music lessons. In 1956, Daddy purchased an old upright piano for our house. When the movers placed it in the living room, I told Momma and Daddy, "I'm going to play that piano." Without much attention or thought, they said, "That's good." They did not know how serious I was. I had been watching my third grade teacher, Mrs. Janie Gardner, as she played the piano for our class devotions. Mrs. Gardner was a master musician. I admired the way she gracefully sat and ran her fingers over the keys. I had watched and prayed and prayed and watched, hoping that one day I would be able to play.

Momma and Daddy left for work. I sat down at the keyboard and prayed real hard, "Lord, let me play this piano." I slowly placed my hands on the keys and it seemed His spirit moved in my fingers as I played. "The Lord has need of workers to till His fields today, so kindly He has led me to walk in wisdom's way; I pray for grace to help me with all my heart to say—O' Blessed Savior, Count on me." I continued at the piano, playing tunes that came to mind. Neighbors began to come in and not long the house was filled with amazed neighbors and friends. They weren't quite as amazed as I or my parents when they returned home from work.

Although Johnnie Mae went sour (pickles) on her music, she still was able to play and would sit often at the piano to play. Jessie and I started playing for churches all across Vicksburg and Warren County. The first time I played for a church, Mt. Pilgrim located up Highway 61 North of Vicksburg, they put two Sears Roebuck Catalogues on the stool to make it convenient for me to reach the keys.

Jessie was particularly fond of Rev. Silas Smith, accessing him to be an honest and devout minister. She played for two of his churches and would often share portions of his sermons with us after services. She loved one of his favorite songs..."It was in my childhood, a many years ago ... in that little wooden church house out on a hill...."

There was always some humor to be found, even in playing for the churches. Jessie sat at the piano at Mt. Carmel, playing through some songs before a play one night. The play, "The Doctor of Correction" written by a stalwart, Christian lady of Vicksburg, Mrs. Rosa Straughter, featured a devil. The characters had all dressed and awaited the seven o'clock curtain time. Jessie knew about the play, was going to play for it, but did not know about the man dressed in the devil suit. Wham! went her fingers across the keys as the devil slowly walked up the side aisle, headed in her direction. The old upright piano rested against the back wall of the high elevated choir stand. The portion of the building additionally sat high from the ground on long stone pillars. The playing continued as did Satan's approach. A touch on the shoulder claims Jessie's attention. She glances back, still playing....Thank God! The usher grabbed the tail of her skirt just before she stepped out of the huge window next to the piano. I forget who they got to play for the program.

I was later informed that Boo (my next oldest brother) had also fainted back in one of the little rooms at the front of the church when he walked in and saw the devil standing there. If anyone needed to faint from the devil's presence it was Boo, the worst of my parents' children. Oh yeah, he was bad—dug deep holes in the ground, filled them with water, covered them over with grass and stuff and called to Daddy, "Come here!" Daddy "fell" for this trick at least twice. Oh yeah, he was bad—went to visit Mr. D. C. Bolden and slipped out into the yard, stalked about twenty-five bitties (baby chickens) and killed them. When Mr. D. C. caught him and asked, "Boy what happened to my chickens?!", Boo replied, "I deadened them!" He had every right to be afraid of the devil. They couldn't whip him because he was epileptic and would go into seizures that we as children called "annegisms." I knew he could fake them if he wanted to.

7

Stories of the Bottom

We liked to sit on the front porch late in the evening and listen to Daddy tell stories. They were all so fascinating as he used much dramatic expression to spell bind us. For example, Daddy said, "There was a man in Vicksburg whose name was Joseph Biedenharhn. One day he was asked to make refreshments for a big summer picnic. He made sandwiches and punch. The punch was so good that people kept asking him for more. Eventually he decided to bottle his punch made with extracts from the coca bean in old canning jars. People laughed at him, said he was crazy and told him nobody would pay a nickel for his punch in an old jelly jar. They were wrong. He had bottled the world's first coca-cola."

In a good mood for storytelling, Daddy continued with his second story as little eyes watched him carefully and little ears perched to hear every word.

Once upon a time, there was an old man who had been ruler of his village for many years. He knew that soon he would die and had to choose one of his three sons to take over as ruler when he died.

His oldest son was big and strong and was a great hunter. The second son was not quite as strong, but was very smart. The third and youngest son was a weak and puny boy. The folks even said he was dumb and stupid. He was different somewhat—he was retarded, stuttered when he spoke.

"How do I decided which of these boys will take over when I die?" the father kept asking himself. Then, it came to him as he sat looking at a gigantic mountain in the distance. "I'll challenge these boys to climb as high up that mountain as they can. The one who climbs highest, I'll name ruler of the village."

He called his first son, the big and strong boy, and said,

46

"Son, put on your mountain-climbing gear. I want you to climb as high up the mountain as you can. Bring me something back for a symbol of how high you climbed."

The big, strong son put on the mountain-climbing gear, left and stayed away for three days. He returned and said, "Father, I have climbed a thousand feet up that mountain and I brought back a stone as a symbol of how high I climbed." His Father was so proud of him. Then he called his second son, the smart boy and said, "Son put on your mountain-climbing gear. I want you to climb as high up that mountain as you can. Bring me something back as a symbol of how high you climbed."

The smart son left home and returned after five days, bringing his Father a twig. He said, "Father I have been a thousand five hundred feet up that mountain. This twig is a symbol of how high I climbed."

The old man was certain that his smart son would take over at this death, but remembered he had another son. He wanted to be fair and had to give him a chance. He called the weak and puny boy, the one the folks said was dumb and stupid and said to him, "Son, put on your mountain-climbing gear. Try to climb up that mountain. Be careful, it's a dangerous mountain. Bring me something back, boy, as a symbol of how high you climbed."

The third son left and stayed away all week. Near the end of the second week, he still had not come back home. His father sat on the front porch crying and blaming himself, "I never should have sent that weak, puny boy to climb the mountain. He has probably fallen to his death," he said.

As the evening shadows fell, he looked into yonder's distance and saw the weak boy slowing walking back to the house. The boy stood at the steps of the porch, looked up at his father and stuttered "Father, I don't have a stone from a thousand feet up that mountain. I don't have a twig from a thousand five hundred feet up that mountain." His father asked compassionately, "Boy, what do you have then?" The son said, "I have been to the top of that mountain and I have a view of the other side. On the other side of the mountain there is a city and it seems like the sun is always shining there."

Daddy stood to walk into the house, but stopped and said, "Always remember that. Don't let anybody tell you what you can't do. Stick to it—you'll make it to the top." Just as he pulled the screen door open, I said, "Daddy why is the Bottom called the Bottom?" He responded, "Because it lies at the foot of several hills. They named it after a white man who owns a lot of houses down here." I fired my next question. "Will we always have to live in the Bottom?" Daddy turned, came over closer and said, "No. Anybody can leave the Bottom, but you don't have to leave to get on top." In childlike manner, I said, "Why?" Daddy found his best answer to end what might have been a night of questions from a child's heart, "One day you will be big enough to understand why and how."

Jessie Clyde (Ray) Chiplin at family store, 1975.

8

"It Takes a Whole Village To Rear a Child"
—An African Adage

"But Daddy, you know how Miss Caesar is, she got us mixed up with some other children!" "If Miss Caesar says she saw you stealing those green plums, she saw you—so get on in there and I'll take care of you later!" Later always came too quick—so did the switch.

Children in the Bottom knew to exercise the Miranda Rights before Miranda. They knew that anything they said could and would be used against them in their parents' court. They knew of only one attorney to call on—"Jesus"!—to the top of their voice — which seemed to invoke their parents' spiritual compassion somewhere near the end of a good whipping. There was absolutely no sound or rational explanation to parents' proclamation to their children—(before a whipping) "This is going to hurt me more than it hurts you!" Oh yeah?! Let's change places!

Whippings were last resorts as old folks' rolling of their eyes, intense stares or verbal cautioning had failed, particularly at church. Things were always funnier at church— like every First Sunday morning when the same fly would light on the same spot of Mr. Fred Thomas' shiny bald head. We could have sworn that as hard as he hit at that fly with his cardboard fan, the fly died if no more than from a near-death experience. Our wooden pew rocked as we desperately tried not to laugh out. Daddy's turning around to look at us didn't make it any better.

Now, you tell me, what were we supposed to do when the preacher's top partial fell out in the heat of his sermon? Or when one of the stoutest women in the church arose to

49

testify and said, "Children, I've grown older now, and I got my *biggest* end behind me!" (Our eyes went straight to her derriere—*big and poked out)* One of my brothers did not get a whipping for laughing, but for wetting his pants.

Children in the Bottom knew what things were funny and what things were not. No one made fun of less fortunate people —we were even forced to call a transient "bag man," commonly referred to as "Buster Barnes"—Mr. Barnes. Mr. Barnes nailed some heavy cardboard together and made himself a shed to sleep in when it was cold. Many times Momma put food into boxes and told us to "carry this to Mr. Barnes." We were kind of afraid of him, perhaps because of his appearance and the fact that he never talked.

The whole community proudly exercised their parental authorities over their neighbors' children—and no one became angry.

WHIPPINGS AND DISCIPLINE AT OUR HOUSE

It would have been to my brothers' and sisters' advantage if Daddy and Momma had not read the Scripture—"Spare the rod, spoil the child." Trust me, there was no spoiling, no sparing of the rod (or whip, or belt or pot or whatever was closest to my parents' hands). The government had not popularized the term—child abuse—and if it had it wouldn't have made a bit of difference. Whippings were never acts of parental disdain, but acts of tough, protective love applied directly to the backside.

WHIPPING RULES

1. You had to go and get your own switch, making sure it was not flimsy.

2. All whippings were explained in advance to avoid confusing the recipient.

3. Best not run—(my parents took some kind of pills that made them swift of feet).

4.   The boys' clothes were always checked to make sure they had not slipped on an extra pair of pants to help prevent wheps on their behinds.

Perhaps you can explain to me how children were expected to "Stop that crying!" while lashes of the belt or switch continued. There seemed to be something scientifically symmetrical in the swinging of the belt or switch.

In case you are wondering why I made reference to my brothers and sisters whippings and not mine—I never got one. I was scared to death of a whipping. No, I promise you, it was not because I was the baby child—rather it owed to my understanding of what things would bring on a whipping and when and where to be bad—and bad I was! There was this perpetual look of innocence on my face and a saintly demeanor that beguiled even the smartest.

The closest I came to getting whipped was the day I rode my homemade wooden wagon off the top of Lummie Street, a tall hill. My parents had told me not to—all the more reason for me to. Somewhere about halfway down the hill, the front wheel ran off and the wagon landed on top of me in a ditch. Cut up and badly bruised, I went home crying, pulling the three-wheeled wagon behind me. Daddy said, "I hope you learned a lesson—when you disobey, bad things can happen to you." I wondered why he didn't whip me, but realized later that the keyloid on my left arm was whipping enough for my life.

BLACK—CAUSE FOR A WHIPPING

Children in Marcus Bottom during the '50s, just as children across the nation, know better than to use profanity in the presence of grown people. Cussing heard by the adults or reported by "blabbermouths" also prompted a good whipping. Additionally, people used soap to wash their children's mouths for using profanity. In addition to a list of four-lettered words that were forbidden, we were not to call anyone a fool. More interestingly, we were not to call anyone black. It was thought to be just as vulgar and degrading as the four-lettered words. Resentment and unacceptance of

51

the word "black" was most dramatically displayed in black segregated public schools and colleges of the South. The "Negro or colored" schools at Vicksburg were no exception. Light-skinned children were always given special attention and more privileges than their darker schoolmates. For instance, they had leading roles in school plays and pageants, particularly the May Day Festivities where the May Day Queen was selected because of her lightness of skin. Other school queens were very light, and dark girls were not even considered. Students with light skin generally were given better grades and did not have to work as hard as darker students. Dark boys were automatically singled out as potentially "bad." Guess who got to lead the line to the lunch room, sit at the front of the class, take names and relish other special favors as teacher's pets? You got it.

Perhaps it would be kind not to crucify teachers and administrators of the past educational society for their sins of color preferences (being color-struck) insofar as they reflected the ideology of the larger society. Black had historically referenced America's—and the world's—notions of evil, witchcraft and superstitions. We were told that it was bad luck for a black cat to cross your path. In such an event, you were instructed to take three steps backward or turn and walk in another direction. Blackjacks were sticks (weapons) used often on black people for infractions or non infractions of the law. The black widow spider was feared as having the most lethal bite of all spiders. The object of many racial slurs and jokes was little black Sambo. They said the boogie man was black. Black girls played with white dolls that were beautiful by all standards of American society; toy manufacturers did not make black dolls. Amusingly enough, the most powerful laxative used by people in Vicksburg was black Draught Syrup. It was counted on for a good workout. I firmly believe that the nation did need a "good inner flushing" to dispel bigotry and hate.

For several centuries in America, blacks had been whipped as slaves by white people, whipped because they were black by white people and whipped by older blacks because they called other blacks "black." I cannot count the number of

52

my playmates and friends who got whippings for calling someone black. Black, then, was not a collective name for African-Americans. It was rather perceived to be a dirty word by Negroes, or colored people, who had been conditioned not to appreciate their African heritage. Television commercials targeted black women and men, promoting Arta Skin Tone Cream and Ambi as products to clear and lighten the skin. Certainly, the straightening comb used to straighten (fry) black people's grease-laden hair was a common household device. Many black women who were not able to have certain white styles straightened into their hair for reasons ranging from hair texture to hair length, opted to purchase wigs—most often identical in style and color to white women's hair styles. I remember that on one visit back down to Mt. Israel, an elderly black lady had received a birthday present through the mail from her son in Chicago—a blonde wig with fluffy bangs and also a beautiful negligee. Not knowing that the negligee was not a "Sunday go to the meeting" dress, she strutted proudly down the aisle, and, picture this, with the bangs turned to the back of her head.

It was not until around 1960 when James Brown shocked the air waves with his recording *Say It Loud, I'm Black and I'm Proud*, that more blacks began to explore and accept their heritage. Brown's song raised the eyebrows of Whites and raised the respectability of blacks. It was a tune easy to dance to, but moreover had a message that took some getting used to. We did!

Afro hairstyles emerged along with the dashiki, an African-style, long, loose, shirt-like garment. Braiding the hair in African tribal fashion replaced dangling plats with bows on the end. Barber shops were hit hard as former close-cut customers, following the style, allowed their hair to grow to extensive lengths.

We were becoming "unAmericanized," we spoke of self identity and we actively surveyed our past. In addition to white America's resentment to our newly accepted identity and appearance, there were many blacks who disdained the acceptance of black as being beautiful. They, in keeping with traditional society, were intimidated by change through the very fear of change. Black men and women who wore Afros and African-style clothing and jewelry, were considered by many to be troublemakers, freedom workers or crazy. Whatever the labels given, we were moving towards what Stevie Wonder described as a "place in the sun" when he wrote:

> Like a long, lonely road, I get weary from the load—moving on, moving on. There's a place in the sun, where there's hope for everyone; where my poor restless heart's got to run; there's a place in the sun and before my life is done, got to find me a place in the sun.

ALRIGHT TO BE BLACK

With so much fuss and resentment about being called black, Daddy chose to share some additional history on black during one of his front porch sessions. Daddy's skin color was very dark. He said:

> People whip their children and wash their mouths out for calling people black. If that's not all confused, don't know what is. I wonder, did Jesus' people get a whipping for calling him Black—He was, you know. In all our churches, they paint pictures of him looking like a white man with long blond hair. According to the Bible, he was short of stature, and calmly in appearance. His feet appeared dark as brass burned in a furnace. I wonder, did Solomon's folks get whipped for calling him black? He even said, "Look not upon me because my face is black, my brothers and sisters were angry with me and made me the keeper of their vineyard, and my own vineyard have I not kept." God called Moses, a man of dark complexion, to go down in Egypt's Land and tell Pharaoh to let the children of Israel go. The children of Israel were also dark-skinned people...Now, if you follow the thing real close, you find out that God, when he made man, was in the Garden of Eden. Check a map of Africa in that geographical location and you'll find the Garden of Eden right there at the banks of the Nile River. The Scriptures say that God scooped up mud and made man. Mud is not white, not on the banks of the Nile—it's real dark. So then, Adam had to have been a Negro-looking man. We are all brothers and sisters, part of one family—the family of mankind and it traces back to Adam and his helpmate, Eve.

54

God loves all colors of people, made every one of them,
Don't go 'round hating folks because their skin color is different. What makes a man is what he is on the inside. People
are confused about the black cat. He is a cat like any other
one. Guess they don't like him because they fear him. You
see, people usually don't like what they cannot understand.

We left that front porch session with new respect and an
appreciation for black and all people. Taking Daddy's words
to heart, I wrote a poem that summarized appreciation and
respect for black.

BLACK CAT
By C. K. Chiplin, May, 1959

Black cat crossed my path today-
I took no steps back, went on my way.

He looked at me and I at him,
Seems he wondered if I was like them.

Daddy said the black cat ain't no bad luck,
Said some people just color struck.

Black cat got a hard life—all nine of them,
People keep a' chasing him out on a limb!

Black cat crossed my path and blinked,
Guess he wondered what did I think...

Was I, like the others who were not wise,
Looking at him through hate filled eyes?

Black cat, black cat, go on your way,
Our paths will cross again someday.

DRAWING BY OMAR

55

9

"Under the Tree"

F̲ew sociologists could ever explain the long-lasting (even to now, 1995) bond of brotherhood that existed among the men who stood "under the tree"—a hang-out spot near the corner of Halls Ferry Road and Lanes Street—just outside Deliah's Dew Drop Inn. It served as a "watchtower" on the ground where black men exchanged ideas, rehashed community news and kept a vigilant, protective eye, safeguarding their community.

The changing of seasons had little effect under the tree, as the stout souls who frequented it made climatic adjustments—in summer a couple of electric fans mounted in the tree made life more comfortable; in winter, a fire in an iron barrel, fueled by scraps of wood or whatever warmed the bodies—much more warming was the camaraderie that dispelled acts of violence and vengeance and permeated the very heart of Marcus Bottom.

The men who hung out under the tree were politically aware. In fact, candidates who aspired to public office (after discriminatory voting barriers were removed), knew the strength of the "under-the-tree men." They worked along with other community organizations to get blacks registered, held forums under the tree for political candidates and provided transportation for people to the polls on election days.

"The Tree," the second home, the community vantage point could be compared to the British Tea Houses. The major difference—tea was not served. Rather, there was wine—cheap wine: Boone's Farm, MD—20/20, Strawberry Hill.

While the "under-the-tree men" consumed alcoholic beverages, they would not allow youngsters to drink with them; more precisely, they reported children to their parents for

"Under the Trees" - In Marcus Bottom, time has not removed those who stand or sit under the trees.

infractions ranging from sneaking a drink to being seen out in the Bottom after the sun went down.

Some of the amenities of home were found right there under the tree—a T.V. set powered by an electric cord that ran over to the cafe, a sofa and straight chairs from houses.

Violence in the community was rare and usually never exceeded an alley fight that ended with those involved brushing off and walking back home together. Every now and then there were rumblings in the shotgun houses—someone getting a whipping.

T. V. COMES TO THE BOTTOM

Around the years 1952 and 1953, we would look up to the top of the hill and see television antennas on the roofs of white folks houses. Our source of house entertainment beyond checkers, jack and balls and the usual childhood games had been the radio and family sing-a-longs. We listened to the radio series of *Amos and Andy* and very often the *Mull Singing Convention*. Family sing-a-longs were led by Momma and Daddy who both had beautiful voices. Momma's was a high-pitched, melodic soprano, and Daddy's was a resonant baritone. Daddy had earlier taught himself music and like his mother, could play the piano.

There was much talk about "the radio that would show pictures"—the black and white T.V. We had heard that some black folks across town had even bought T.V. sets. Then, our back door neighbor, Mr. Johnny Carey and his wife, Leola caused quite a stir when they bought an RCA television. That elevated them to something like a royal position, a position of respect and honor in Marcus Bottom.

If anyone deserved a T.V., it was Johnny Carey, for he was a hard-working man who, as I remember, walked to work downtown every day. In keeping with the tradition of sharing, Mr. Johnny would turn his T.V. around to the raised window and turn up the volume. It was summer and the neighbors came from everywhere, bringing chairs to sit and watch—*The Hit Parade, I Love Lucy, The Little Rascals,* and to be sure—*Amos and Andy*!

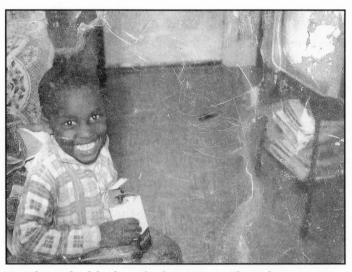

Watching the black and white TV at Chip's house.

Everything went well with "community T.V.," that was until the night of the big boxing match. Mr. Johnny loved boxing—lived boxing! It rained that night, so the T.V. was not turned to the window. Male friends and buddies gathered to watch the match at the Careys' home. After a few commercials promoting Chevrolet and Camel Cigarettes, the televised match was on. Most people sat a distance from Johnny Carey because he often became physically engrossed in boxing matches. This night was no exception. In fact, it was his worst ever. As the punches flew in the ring, so did Johnny Carey's. The boxing intensified—so did Johnny Carey. "Mr. Johnny's opponent" threw a sprinting left hook! Across the room Mr. Johnny flew—right up to the T.V. and landed a devastating blow with his right fist to the side of the T.V.—back to the old radio.

I was in the second grade at Lanes Hill Elementary School. We stood to sing the daily school closing song, "Look to the right, look to the left, before you cross the street—look for the cars, look for the trucks before you cross the street! Goodbye teacher!" Off we flew—headed to Marcus Bottom—a good distance away. Certainly, in keeping with not doing as our parents had asked, we walked through the bayou—a short cut—sleezed with slime and other bayou stuff.

We came up from the bayou on to Halls Ferry Road. We walked on past Jimmy Chu's Grocery and as I looked in the near distance—there it was—a T.V. antenna sprouting from the top of our house in Smith's Alley. Did I run?! Olympic style!

I shall never forget the swelling music as *The Little Rascals* came on. I wondered why Buckwheat was always taken advantage of. I wondered why his was the only hair to stand up on his head when the group was frightened. I wondered why he referred to Alfalfa as "Master Alfalfa." I was becoming racially aware. I remembered that at the end of each *Little Rascals* show, the theme played as the gang marched. The voice of one of the white children called loudly out to Buckwheat, "Buckwheat, you out of step!" He, trying to keep up with the beat would reply, "T'ain't me, hits them!"

He was on target in terms of the black man's steady march for justice and equality—it was not the black man out of step, it was the masses in America who kept pace with the doleful drumbeats of discrimination.

Daddy would not allow us to watch cowboy and Indian shows. He said they were not historically accurate, that Indians in America were not really Indians and they, the Native Americans, had a right to defend their land against the white man's invasion. Additionally, we were forbidden to watch *Tarzan*. Daddy said it was an insult to our African ancestors. He resented seeing hundreds of black people, called JuJu's, running scared by Tarzan's jungle cries. Most other shows were approved for our viewing—*Leave It To Beaver, Ozzie and Harriet, The Hit Parade Farther Knows Best, I Love Lucy*, etc.

"WHITE WATER"

Up to around 1959, city buses ran in Vicksburg. As was the law of the South, blacks paid their money up front, then walked to the rear door and were seated in the "colored section." In the summer of 1954, Momma carried me downtown with her. We put in our dimes and went to the back. As I sat there observing people on the bus, I said, "Momma, you look almost white, you should sit up closer to the front!" She pinched me and said, "All of us colored people have to sit in our place." I remained silent for the duration of the bus ride.

We exited the bus and walked past a number of stores on Washington Street. Momma stopped often and looked at clothes and other things in display windows. Then, we went into the Kress Store. Again my inquiry could not be contained as I saw two water fountains. I slowly read the signs above the fountains. "W-h-i-t-e—White; C-o-l-o-r-e-d—Colored." "Momma, what's the difference in white water and colored water?" Looking around to make sure no one was watching, Momma replied, "Why don't you drink out of both of them, and you'll see." I drank from the colored fountain, then the white fountain, as Momma's protective eyes watched. "They the same!" I blurted. Momma stooped

DRAWING BY MICHAEL ALEXANDER

down and put her hand on my face and instructed, "Charles, there is no difference in the water, the difference is the color of your skin."

That was the moment of truth of my life. Now, it all came into place—colored folks were supposed to be separated from white folks; that's why the white folks live at the top of the hill and we live in the Bottom; that's why Buckwheat calls Alfalfa, "Master Alfalfa."

LIFE GOES ON (SO DOES THE BUS)

My realization of color differences did not change life in the Bottom, it just made it more understandable. I was supposed to act like a colored boy living in a colored community. I pondered what it would feel like to be white—how would things be different? I knew: if I was white, I would live at the top of the hill, but then I could no longer have my good friends: Lou up the Alley, Janice Lee, Rita, Joe

61

Tolliver, Ronald, Betty, Dotty, Joe Scott, Barbara and David Summers up on Alma Street and all the others in the Back Alley. It wasn't worth it.

The next school year arrived, and I was in the third grade. After finally completing the second grade at Lanes Hill (I failed first grade because I was scared of the teacher), I went to McIntyre Elementary—Junior High School—much farther away from home.

There were no school buses for black children. We walked to school on the "colored side" of the street while white children rode past us on school buses, calling us "niggers" and throwing wads of spit wet paper. At least we were able to start school in September like the white children. Up in the Delta of Mississippi where there was much cotton, black schools did not start until around the last of October or whenever all the cotton was harvested—picked by black folks.

After about a month of walking to and from school, Jessie and I started riding the city bus to school in the morning and riding home on the city bus sometimes in the evening.

The bus issue was very sensitive to me. I was bent on breaking the "law." I wanted to see what would happen if I sat down up front. I stood at the bus stop on the corner of Cherry and Openwood streets. My book bag weighed heavy upon my back as did the thought of sitting at the front of the bus. There it was! The city bus. It stopped. The familiar smell of diesel permeated the air and the whoosh of air brakes engaged signaled my strides towards the opening front door. Cling! My dime was inserted. I nervously placed my hands in the front straps of my book bag and walked to the second seat behind the driver. Whoosh! The bus stopped. "Boy you can't sit up here!" the middle-aged white bus driver said as he glared at me through his rearview mirror. I said nothing. I had no idea what was about to happen.

The bus pulled off in a hurry. We did not travel the normal bus route. I was driven down to the police station. The bus driver turned, pointed his finger at me and yelled, "Get off!"

As I walked from the police station to Marcus Bottom, I

wondered what would Momma and Daddy say if they knew what I had done. Well... didn't matter, I was going to do the same thing tomorrow.

Tomorrow and I once more stood and waited for the city bus. Ditto, I sat in the same spot on the bus, once more the bus headed for the police department. This time however, the driver escorted me inside the station and proclaimed, "This boy is a troublemaker!" He explained why he had brought me there. The officer on the desk asked for my telephone number. I told him my parents were at work. "Where?!" he insisted and I said, "Daddy is at Vicksburg Paint and Glass Company." He called and it was not long until Daddy was there to get me.

Daddy's words to me were few enroute to Marcus Bottom, but they were meaningful. "Son, I know its wrong for them to treat us like this, but that's the way it is right now. One day all of this is going to change; you might even end up driving one of those buses, but for now, I'm trying to keep a roof over your head and food on the table. My boss will fire me if you keep it up."

I didn't want Daddy to lose his job, so I stopped riding the bus. That perhaps was just as bad for as I walked home daily my hostility grew, grew as I saw the bus passing with white people seated comfortably up front and "colored folks" packed in the back; grew as the white children's yellow school bus passed and they shouted slurs; grew as I walked off the normal route, just around the block on Monroe Street and saw a sign in the window of the Glass Kitchen that read—"Whites Only." I did my usual mental calculations and there I was—inside the Glass Kitchen, with my book satchel on my back, with my black face. "We ain't looking for no help," the white lady working behind the counter said. "I want a coca cola," I replied. "We can't serve you in here!", she responded and continued, "What's your name?" "Charles Kinnard Chiplin," I proudly told her and walked on out of the door. How she found out who my parents were or where they worked still confuses me to this day. That night, Momma and Daddy called me to the front room and Daddy said, "Sit down. We know what you did today, you can't keep doing that, these folks will kill you boy." Momma added, "I don't know what would happen to me if you came up like that boy Emmet Till." I had seen the picture of the brutalized body of Emmet Till and had often been unable to sleep for bleak memories of his horror story in Money, Mississippi. Emmet had come from Chicago to spend the summer with his uncle in Money and was not aware of Southern hostilities towards black people. He had told a white lady, "Bye, baby" as he left a store, and his body, appearing like a monster, had been dragged from the Tallahatchie River with a gin mill fan chained to his neck. My parents' point was clear, and I tried to resign myself to act like a colored boy should.

It wasn't too long after that that we saw on the news that a black lady named Rosa Parks had refused to give up her seat to a white man in Montgomery, Alabama. She was arrested, and the NAACP, led by a young preacher named Rev. Dr. Martin L. King, had initiated a boycott against the bus line of Montgomery. I was greatly relieved that somebody else had taken a stand against wrong and hoped for the day that black people could ride up front on the buses of Vicksburg.

10

"Jim, You're Fired"

My episodes with the bus and The Glass Kitchen did not get my father fired from Vicksburg Paint and Glass Company, but Daddy's strong belief in equality did. In 1955, several black men in Vicksburg, along with my father, signed a petition that stated: "We, the undersigned, want our children to receive an equal education..." Separate, but equal had surfaced as the nation's placation to vast social injustices. To be sure, facilities, particularly educational facilities, were separate, but by no means equal.

We received textbooks that had been used for at least 10 years by white students. We did not know what a science laboratory looked like; our school band marched in white shirts and black pants while the white schools had uniforms; our football team received dirty, worn-out football suits after the white teams had used them many years. Daddy and his colleagues were very aware of our educational depravation and had mustered the nerve to petition the school board for immediate changes. Their petition, bearing only five names, was published in the *Vicksburg Evening Post*, and read: "We, the undersigned, request that our children receive an equal education to that available to white children in the Public Schools of Vicksburg."

Mr. Cox, the owner of Vicksburg Paint and Glass, called Daddy in and asked him to have a retraction of his name published or he would have to fire him. Daddy shared, "I told Mr. Cox, I can't do that because I do want Edward Lee, Johnnie Mae, James, Jr., Jessie and Charles to get an equal education—they deserve that much!" He was fired.

Cutting glass, climbing ladders, and putting in windows had become Daddy's life. He was a master at his trade and had also earlier taught his boss the art of glazing.

There was an unusual calm in our shotgun house when Daddy came in and announced that he had been fired. Momma was quick to say, "That's alright, Chiplin, we'll make it; we all have to pull together."

That night, our song for the family sing-a-long reinforced the family's faith and sparked hope during what was to be a bad economic time.

> "Like a ship that's tossed and driven, battered by an angry sea— when the storms of life are raging and their fury falls on me; I wonder what I have done, to make this race so hard to run; then I say to my soul—take courage, for the Lord will make a way somehow."

Determination was a key factor of survival in Marcus Bottom, and most assuredly in our household. There would be no more Friday paycheck, but there would be continued light bills, water and gas bills, house notes and the need for food on the table.

Daddy had the skills and management abilities to run his own glass shop. Several blocks up on Halls Ferry Road, Mr. Johnson ran a mechanic shop. He offered him a large section of the building to start his business, "Jim's Glass Shop."

We were so proud of Daddy and pitched in to help set up the shop. Everything just seemed to come together—he found a black 1947 Ford truck that was in good shape, built the glass racks that were needed, bought his initial glass inventory and had his business signs painted both on the building and the truck. Finally, he had everything but customers. Many people who had called on him for services while he worked at Vicksburg Paint and Glass passed on by and took their business to his former employer. There was however, enough patronage to keep his doors open for a while.

Daddy was one of a very few people skilled in resilvering mirrors—a tedious chemical process. This skill brought him some white customers: people who had expensive antiques and preferred the authenticity of the original glass.

Momma took a job cooking in the cafeteria of All Saints Episcopal College out on Military Avenue. She proved to be a valuable asset to her supervisor, a white lady, Mrs. Hazel Tennant. Mrs. Tennant seemed to be from a different place and time and treated black people with much respect. Feeling very close to our family, she instructed us to call her "grandmother." Momma's superior food preparation, decorating and "spreading" skills won her great acclaim, not only at All Saints, but throughout the city of Vicksburg. She had even worked earlier at The Old Southern Tea Room, (a then "White Only") restaurant where southern belles and gents frequented to relish what was to be one of the last vestiges of white southern domain and black servitude. She quit because of her resentment of being required to wear the "Aunt Jemima" red and white head rag.

Fringe benefits of food from All Saints College to some extent compensated for the low salary Momma received. Her income, along with Daddy's meager profits from the glass shop, pulled us through, but was not enough to sustain my brother, Edward Lee, who had transferred from Alcorn College to Tougaloo. Without the present "luxuries" of government-sponsored grants and loans, there just was not enough money for Edward to continue, and he withdrew after his sophomore year.

The sparks of freedom, justice and equality that were fanned by my parents ignited in him and he was arrested not far from Alcorn, back down in Fayette, Mississippi. Somehow he felt that his recent conversion to Catholicism merited his right to attend the white Catholic Church in Fayette. Was he ever wrong! Edward had scarcely said the "Hail Mary" and made the sign of the cross when several white policemen entered the front door of the church and beckoned for him. He was placed under arrest and carried to the Fayette Jail. My mother's sister's husband, Uncle Red, bailed him out.

Not long after his arrest, Edward Lee enlisted in the Army, vowing not to return to the South. To this date he has not, except for brief vacations.

11

"There's a Thrill Up on the Hill"
(NEGRO EDUCATION IN VICKSBURG)

For many years, Bowman High School in Vicksburg was rated among the top colored high schools in the state. The three-story, stately brown brick building stood sprawling at the top of one of the steepest hills in Vicksburg, Bowman Street. It was comparatively a good school, although like other black, "separate but not equal" schools, it lacked educational equipment, library books and most things to enhance education. The fact that Bowman High went through the 12th grade made it appealing to numerous black students across the state whose high schools stopped at the 10th grade.

Momma's sister, Johnnie Mae (Aunt Shug) and Ruth Hall (who later was married to our Uncle, Edward) attended Bowman High. They were determined to complete their public school educations in spite of having to leave Fayette where the school also stopped at 10th grade.

They often shared school day stories from Bowman and spoke of Professor James A. Bowman, for whom the school was named. Professor Bowman was reputedly a strict disciplinarian and considered education to be serious business. He demanded respect and got it without saying a word. Professor Bowman controlled hallways filled with students, monitored classrooms and maintained order in the school's cafeteria without saying a word, according to reports. Aunt Shug said he "spoke softly and carried a big stick."

Daddy was almost dismissed from Aunt Shug's and Ruth's graduation for blurts of laughter due to his whispered dialogue with Momma Lucy who sat next to him. "Son, why that man keep looking at me?" Daddy shrugged his shoulders, taking her question lightly. "Up there, son, he has not

Temple High School

taken his eyes off me since I sat down!" "Momma Lucy, you probably just imagining that....shhhh" "It ain't my magination, look son, up in that window, he got his eyes stuck on me!" Daddy looked as Momma Lucy nervously pointed to a picture of Professor Bowman located above the stage. "See there, I told you, he got his eyes peered on me, watching me like a hawk watch a chicken!" Daddy later surmised that people could be controlled by even a picture of Professor Bowman.

ABOUT STUDENT CONTROL AND RESPECT

Not only did students respect Professor Bowman, they had a genuine high regard for teachers and other school personnel. They were quite aware that disorderly conduct led to punishment which included a whipping by the teacher and/or principal and at least one more whipping from parents when they went home, the chance of being seated on a high stool ("dunce stool") in the front corner of the room, extensive physical exercises and suspended participation from school activities. Any one of the previous brought on subsequent ridicule (teasing) from other students. As a result, disorderly behavior was minimal. Without fail, fights were reserved to the end of the school year, usually down the street from the school. Those who fought were cheered on by student spectators. With the fight over—eyes blackened, noses bloody, clothes torn, hair pulled, faces scarred—students walked on home together. No one pulled a gun or knife. Within days, if not the same evening, the fighters were back together. There was obviously little choice, for they lived in the same communities that were closely linked together in love. Their parents were associates if not friends who strove together for mutual survival.

Respect also was relative to the teachers' parental roles in their students' lives. They counseled, talked to, reprimanded and encouraged their students. They talked about life and the guts it took to live it well. They spoke of the challenges ahead for black girls and boys who, even with a good education, would live in America's second-class society. They spoke of God and led their students in morning devotional exercise—a song, prayer, pledge to the flag and a closing song.

"THERE'S A THRILL UP ON THE HILL"

Bowman High was changed to an elementary school after the new school, Rosa A. Temple, was completed. Temple High was the capstone of black schools, the epitome of segregated excellence, and the cause for much bragging by black people in Vicksburg. Like Boman, it set high up on a hill. Typically, it was built across the railroad tracks in a black community. Didn't matter. It was our new school and we proudly accepted our mascot (Buccaneers!) and wore the school colors—green and white, just as proudly.

Mr. Sanders, Professor Bowman's successor at Bowman High, was principal of Temple and was assisted by a young man, recently out of college, James E. Stirgus. Shortly after moving to Temple High, Sanders retired and Stirgus became principal. He inherited a dedicated faculty and employed numerous other young teachers just completing college.

The quality of education provided by the Temple instructors was very good although educational resources were still limited and not comparable to white schools. The human resources were second to none. Miss Thelma J. Watson, a senior English literature instructor, became a living legend through her instructional prowess. Her sharp ability to rhyme and joke while maintaining tight discipline, endeared her to the students. She taught her classes with the same fiery spirit with which she led the school's pep rallies. Tall of stature, kind of heart, and strong of mind, Miss Watson literally performed in her classes and ignited academic sparks in her students. Learning long passages from William Shakespeare and Edgar Allen Poe seemed trivial to the many students who wanted to emulate her. "A Psalm of Life," "Prologue to the Canterbury Tales," descriptions of Canterbury Tale characters, closing lines of Thanatopsis, Poe's "Bells," Kipling's "If," Guest's "Myself," and scores of other literary works were memory assignments along with learning dialogue and character portrayals for class theatrical performances.

Just down the hall from Miss Watson was my mother's sister-in-law, Mrs. Dunlap. The motto posted on her door summarized her rigid educational philosophy—"If you are not here for business, you have no business here!" She used down-home, sometimes country phrases to get her point across and thereby constantly engaged the attention of her students in 11th grade English. Each of the dedicated teachers had his/her trademark and was remembered for life. In Vicksburg, the names Banks, Parrott, Connor, Tripplett, Nelson, Madison, Grimmett, Howard, Green, Knox, Tillman, Prentiss, Crump, Ferguson, DuBois, Wesley, Douglas, Hughes, Otis, Fletcher, Smith, McIntyre, Temple, Austin and Pickett stand out on the long list of high school teachers who made a difference in the lives of scores of black students.

Yes, there was "a thrill up on the hill" not only in terms of academic achievement, but in many other things, particularly sports. The Buccaneer football and basketball teams long time championship records garnered respect even from opposing schools—Jim Hill, Lanier, Brinkley, Coleman High, Sadie V. Thompson and others. Our coaches used the same motivational tools as our instructors and were respected as big brothers and in many instances, fathers. They taught fairness and what it takes to be a winner: the courage to accept defeat unbroken in spirit. Athletes were expected to

71

achieve academically and in Miss Watson's room and most other teachers' rooms, to no lesser degree than other students. In fact, Miss Watson assigned extra passages to athletes, particularly if we lost a game. For instance — "Let others cheer the winning man, there's one I hold worthwhile, 'tis he who does the best he can, then loses with a smile. Beaten, he is, but not to stay down with the rank and file. That man will win some other day who loses with a smile."

Our parents were just as enthusiastic and excited about athletic competition as we were and showed up for games not only at our school, but all over the state. Daddy was elected president of the Buccaneer Fan Club and worked tirelessly with Mrs. T. P. Williams, an ardent supporter and instructor and many other loyal parent fans.

"Blueberry Hill," a 1950s tune of Fats Domino, was arranged for the Buccaneer Band by Mr. L. W. (Jiving) Jones. Mr. Jones, "Jiving Jones," lived and breathed music and was largely responsible for the success of the Buccaneer Marching Band. He played at times with the nationally famous Red Tops, a pop, swing, jazz group composed of excellent black musicians. Jiving Jones, in like manner, organized some of his best high school musicians into a group called the Swing Masters.

While there were many bragging rights associated with the academic and athletic programs of Vicksburg, there still were few civil rights granted black people. Our educational "great white fathers," in keeping with tradition, continued to make every effort to insult and degrade our educational institutions. Having endured the issuing of worn out, hand-me-down books and other things from the white schools, many black parents were angered when Mr. Cooper, the superintendent of Vicksburg Schools, sent Temple the smelly and dirty football and band suits. A group of rallying, angry black mothers including Annette Fox, and naturally, Rosa L. Chiplin, led by Mrs. Lee Willa Miller, converged on Mr. Cooper's office and made it emphatically clear that our team members would not make one huddle nor advance the ball towards the goal line in Cooper's old suits and the Buccaneer Band would not make one formation wearing them either. They were told that no funds were available to purchase new suits for the team and band, and left with the thunderous determination to raise money and buy suits themselves. And they did!

Yes there were and had been many thrills on two hills in Vicksburg—Bowman and Temple. Even before the new high school was built, the hill where Temple stood was Lanes Hill Elementary School. Mr. J. R. Stampley, one of Mississippi's legendary educators, was principal. Mr. Stampley was a colorful, charismatic man who had the rare ability to get people involved in things. He, like my father, was affiliated with numerous social and civic organizations. Unlike some black administrators of that period, he was a lifelong member of the National Association for the Advancement of Colored People.

Not only was there education on the hills for blacks in Vicksburg, there was education down the hill—down Cherry Street at McIntrye Elementary and Junior High School. Mr. O. W. Howard was principal. He too "ran a tight ship," with determined and dedicated teachers including Mrs. Rebecca Vaughn, T. P. Williams, Sarah Ewell, Ollie Shirley, Middleton, Ledora Marley, Myrlie Polk, Janie Gardner, Arlene Thomas, Ruby Tripplet, Coleman/Murrey, Alma Brown, Corine Marshall, Marshall, Atlanta Hicks, Alice Hicks, Clay and others.

Black teachers worked hard in their efforts to prepare black students for America's color-conscious society as they also were victims of injustice and discrimination. One of their most dramatic yearly experiences of racism was preparation for the state teachers meeting. Black teachers attended their separate teachers association on the campus of Jackson State College and later at Mississippi Coliseum. Neither their high respect as educators nor their professional degrees negated that they were "colored teachers" and bound to the same degrading segregated traditions as other blacks.

Since black teachers, just as other blacks, could not try on clothes in stores, many of them shopped at Lula Belle's, a women's clothing store which was located near the campus of Jackson State College. Lula Belle's business was brisk each year, as black teachers drove from across the state to make purchases for the teachers' meeting. Female teachers used the event as a fashion fair, sporting brightly colored dresses, fine shoes and wide, flowery hats.

All dressed up, the teachers met in Jackson for two days in intensely emotional sessions enhanced through the singing of southern gospel music and sometimes a good sermon. Theirs was a mighty bond of love, hope and courage—love for their students, hope for a better day to come and courage enough to keep working although shadowed beneath the evils of southern discrimination. I am sure they shared with their colleague, T. J. Watson the belief that, "Lives of great men all remind us, we can make our lives sublime, and, in departing, leave behind us—footprints on the sands of time. Footprints that perhaps another, sailing o'er life's solemn main, a forlorned or shipwrecked brother, seeing may take heart again..."(From "A Psalm of Life").

The serious and not so serious students were challenged and made it. Photograph by Johnston Photography.

12

Johnnie's Story

Our family had established quite a respectable reputation in Marcus Bottom and Vicksburg. Daddy was the strong, black gentleman and businessman. Momma was the pretty, witty, loving lady who shared freely with everybody. The Chiplin children were mannerable, did well in school and were talented. And then, the bombshell hit, stirring rumor and whispers all over the place. "Mr. Chiplin's gal pregnant!" "They tell me, I don't know if its much truth to it or not, but Johnnie Mae Chiplin pregnant, and she ain't but a girl herself." "You know she gonna have to marry to give that baby a last name!;" "I could tell by the way her eyes looked the last time I saw her, that she musta stomped her toe—what a shame!;" "She ain't even finished Bowman High! What she gonna do with a baby? Poor Rosa (Momma), gonna have to raise that baby for her!"—were fragments of the whisperings (gossiping) around Marcus Bottom.

Yes, Johnnie Mae, Daddy's darling girl, just turning 14, was going to have a baby. Drawing from their deep inner strength, Momma and Daddy weathered the storms of lashing of holier-than-thou tongues that served as Johnnie's "judges and jury," sentencing her, in their estimation, to a life of shame, hard work and alienation.

Daddy's questions to Johnnie were direct after it was certain she was pregnant—a fact she never tried to hide. "What are your plans?" "Who is the child's father?" Johnnie informed him that she wanted to have her baby and go on with her education, and that Sherman Jackson, an older guy who lived in the neighboring Douglas Park Community, was the child's father.

Johnnie's situation was bleak. During that period, young ladies who had given birth to children could not return to

75

Sherman stands on porch of house on Lane's Street shortly after marriage to Johnnie.

The eyes of anticipation—a child of the Bottom is captured in this 1957 photo of Sharon, Johnnie Mae's daughter.

public school and were asked to turn in their choir robes and figuratively "wear the scarlet letter." Johnnie did turn in her choir robe, but she refused to wear the scarlet letter. More precisely, she adorned a cloak of pride. Daddy and Momma insisted that her home education continue. Math, English, history, foreign languages and the like were included in her daily assignments, monitored firmly by Daddy. Within four months she and Sherman were married. Sitting one day on our front porch, reading the newspaper (an unwritten rule of my father's), she saw an advertisement for the General Education Development (GED) Test at Alcorn College in Lorman, Mississippi. Not long after the simple wedding (before a Justice of the Peace) and reception at our house, she went to Alcorn, took the test, and passed it.

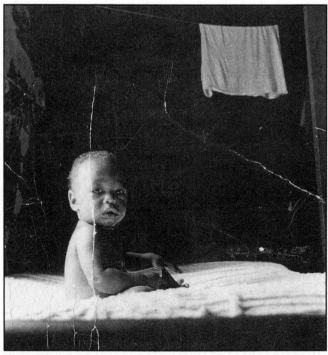

Grandson Marcus, now Dr. Marcus Jackson owner of Jackson Dental Clinics, sits on the bed waiting for his diaper to dry.

After Billy, her first child was born, she enrolled in the Licensed Practical Nurse Course at Kuhn Memorial Hospital in Vicksburg and graduated. For five years, she worked as an LPN for the Sisters of Mercy Hospital, also in Vicksburg.

Sherman moved in with us and worked on various labor jobs for short periods of time. According to Johnnie, "I had a problem with seeing Daddy leave every morning for work, while Sherman many times remained at home, sleeping past noon. We separated in about nine months. I went back to him several times and we gave birth to five more children."

With six children and barely turning twenty-one, Johnnie went to Hinds Community College in Raymond, Mississippi, studied, and became a registered nurse.

By now, the rumor on Johnnie Mae Chiplin Jackson had changed. "Johnnie Mae done made something out of herself;" "I knew all along that girl would make it!," etc. Johnnie's determination and self-will were attributable to the lessons instilled by our parents and their identification of roads from the bottom.

Her in-and-out relationship with Sherman never diminished her determination. The years before she was able to afford her first car (a used 1957 Chevrolet), she walked, usually with a baby across her shoulder and five "little stair steppers" tagging at her coat-tail. She and the children had long since moved to a shotgun house on Lane Street, not too far from our house. There was no restroom inside the house. The string of over 10 little rustic shotgun houses shared one restroom (outhouse) built behind the houses. As her relationship with Sherman continued off and on, he was rarely there to assist with the children and they stayed with us or my father's mother (Anney) while Johnnie worked.

Not once during her difficult years did she apply for social assistance (welfare, government food programs—"commodity," —there were no food stamps). "I knew I had a great responsibility with or without Sherman; Billy, Linda, Sharon, Gerald, Rose and Marcus had to be taken care of. I did not want Daddy, the government or anybody else taking on my load," Johnnie shared.

78

Later years, by 1972, would signal the formal end of her marriage to Sherman. They were divorced after he jumped on her for bringing his dinner home from a restaurant after she and my sister Jessie, had been shopping.

Reflecting on her early experiences, Johnnie said, "I love my children, but if I had to do it over, I would have waited later to have them. It was hard on me. Daddy would not let me leave my babies with Momma. If I wanted to attend an event, they had to go with me. Most of the time I stayed at home. You miss so much of your childhood when you have a baby and you are only a child yourself. I found out right quick that a baby is not a toy or thing, but is an individual who must be provided for, loved and protected."

13

Oh Freedom Over Me

Daddy informed us that there was going to be a Civil Rights Meeting over at Wesley Methodist Church on a Saturday evening in June, 1962. Without question, we would be there.

Walking into the sanctuary, I heard the persuasive voice of a black man leading the few people there in a song.

> "Oh Freedom, Oh Freedom, Oh Freedom over me— And before I be a slave, I'll be buried in my grave and go home to my Lord and be free!"

The guy in charge of the meeting introduced two white people who had come with him from somewhere up North and informed that numerous other freedom workers would soon be coming to Vicksburg. Not long into the meeting, Daddy stood and made our out-of-town guests welcome. "Vicksburg is a strange place—it was the last stronghold of the Confederacy, and today, over 100 years later, it is still behind. It won't be easy here in Vicksburg for you, but if it's anything I or my family can do, just let me know!" he shared.

Within several weeks other freedom workers had come to town—organizers for the Student Nonviolent Coordinating Committee (SNCC). They appeared as heroes of sort, for they had the nerve even to suggest that change was imperative. They looked "different" in regards to how others in the community looked. The white guys were not clean shaven and some had long, flowing hair—hippie type. The black men had beards and Afros.

They were labeled swiftly as "outside agitators," "hippies," "flower children," and the like. Those of us who met them at the first meeting saw and respected them as

"Freedom Workers," young people giving up their summers to help us.

Telephones started buzzing around Vicksburg with the news of "Freedom Workers" in town. "But, why they come to Vicksburg?"; "We doing alright here;" "They must be trying to tear up our town!;" "Aren't there enough problems up North for them?" —were questions and comments carried via telephone and street conversations.

Some blacks in Vicksburg relished an unusual sense of satisfaction and would rather have left things as they were—no blacks on the fire, sheriff's or police departments; no blacks employed at City Hall except as maids or janitors; positively no blacks working in department stores, except in domestic or service positions; schools remained segregated; city services to black neighborhoods were substandard if not nonexistent; most blacks were not registered to vote. Yet, some blacks questioned, "Why don't they (Civil Rights Workers) leave us alone?!"

Borrowing the words of William Tripplet, a longtime black resident of Vicksburg and educator, "There had been a thundering silence in the Hill City." He, along with a limited number of other black teachers, was not afraid to attend meetings and speak out.

Words of "the Freedom Movement" at first had little impact on Marcus Bottom. People in the Bottom traditionally held a "wait and see" attitude. "If it changes— good, if not—we'll live on", seemed to be the prevailing pulse. Not for Jim Chiplin. Something about that first meeting erupted a drive within him.

"Rosa, there are more Freedom Workers headed to Vicksburg and the several who are already here are having trouble finding a place to stay. I was thinking we could let some of them stay with us," I recall Daddy speaking to Momma on a Saturday morning in July of 1962. "If what we have can help out a little, I don't see why not", Momma responded and continued after a moment of deliberate hesitation. "We will be taking a chance, though." "We slipped away from Jake Wagoner's didn't we?" Daddy quizzed and they both laughed.

Within a few days, three Civil Rights workers moved in with us: a young white lady, Renae, about 20; a black guy, Robert, about 22; and a white guy, David, about 24. Renae played the guitar very well. The first night with us, after almost sinful proportions of Momma's dinner, we sat in the living room and joined with Renae and the others singing, "Michael row the boat ashore, Hallelujah, Michael row the boat ashore; Hallelujah." Several other songs followed, but I was particularly taken with the following Peter, Paul and Mary song.

> How many roads must a man walk down, before you call him a man? How many seas must the white dove sail before she sleeps in the sand? How many times must the cannons be fired, before they're forever banned? The answer my friend, is blowing in the wind; the answer is blowing in the wind.

David had driven his Volkswagen to Vicksburg and provided transportation assistance for the movement. The dull gray Volkswagen puttered from the load of baggage and sometimes up to five people as David scurried about Vicksburg knocking on doors and meeting people. Many times, he shared, "People would come to the door, ask if I was the insurance man and when I said 'No, I am David, a Civil Rights worker'... they slammed the door in my face."

David was a genuine humanitarian with a brilliant sharp mind. He had developed superior journalism skills and immediately collaborated with Mrs. Dilla Irvin, Dr. Aaron Shirley, his wife Ollie, and some others to start a community newspaper called *The Vicksburg Citizen's Appeal.* Up to that time, blacks were only mentioned in the Vicksburg newspaper if they had committed a crime. For a while Mr. O. W. Hoard, principal of McIntyre School, had written a column of the paper called "Among Colored Folks." "Among Colored Folks" carried brief news accounts and announcements for the black community. Titles (Mr. and Mrs.) were never printed with the names of black people in the newspaper or the telephone directory. (Telephone listings of black people were obvious because whites were listed as Mr. or Mrs.)

Working out of a spare room at Mrs. Irvin's house, David

and others, including myself, spent many long hours preparing for the first edition. With it finished, we were ecstatic, knowing that at last, a mechanism for spreading the truth throughout Vicksburg was in place and ready to hit the streets. It did, largely through the efforts of Mr. Pink Taylor who served as circulation manager. Mr. Pink proudly loaded the bundles of papers on the back of his pickup truck and headed to prearranged dispatch locations.

To acquaint people with the paper, most of the first edition copies were given away. There was generally good reception with some criticisms and speculation.

In addition to a new, controversial newspaper, our Civil Rights friends began efforts to open a "freedom school." Talk of the proposed freedom school gave rise to the following questions:

1. Who needs another school in Vicksburg?
2. What can they teach different at a "freedom school?"
3. How will they get accreditation?
4. Where will they put the school?
5. Who will pay for it?

In one of the strategy meetings for the freedom school, the previous questions were very well answered. First, "Who needs a freedom school?" Scores of black and white children had been "miseducated" in segregated schools and taught to consider race as a prerequisite for hatred and separation. "What can they teach different at a freedom school?" Historical truths that had been excluded from public school textbooks...i.e. contributions of blacks in science, medicine, astronomy, and building of the world's empires and great cities. "How will they get accreditation?" Accreditation was not as much an issue as an inclusive education. "Where will they put the school?" Wherever there was a facility willing to accept the school. "Who will pay for it?" Collective community participation, with instructional services provided by volunteers.

David approached my father one afternoon at our house concerning the freedom school. Daddy responded, "I have charge of the old Baptist Academy building. We (the Sunday School Convention where he served as President) have been doing a lot of work up on that hill to bring the old building up to standard. I think it would be a good spot for the freedom school." Immediately, Daddy, along with several other convention members began to make special preparations to house the freedom school. David and other freedom workers pitched in to help restore the old wood frame, two-story, building located up on a high hill just off Openwood Street near the northern limits of Vicksburg. The building was nearly 85 years old and had been constructed just after the Civil War in Vicksburg. Its construction was sound and stately. Naturally it bore the marks and deterioration of many years, but, it was available and had much potential.

The group of workers, led by my father, worked diligently for nearly a month. I remember Daddy stopping to rest one day, after Momma had brought food for the workers and they were sitting down at an old upright in a room of the building. After taking a rag and dusting off the keys, he began to play and sing: "O' Lord my God, when I in awesome wonder, consider all the worlds Thy hands have made"....Others gathered around the piano and joined in the chorus, "Then sings my soul, my Savior God to Thee, How great Thou art, How great Thou art." At the end of several choruses, Daddy said, "God is great and He is doing a great thing through you freedom workers...it's a lot of people don't like it, but just hold on a little while longer." Having spoken, he went back to work on the building.

On the same night, David and seven other freedom workers had come home (to our house) to rest from the long day's work. As Momma prepared dinner, the telephone rang. Momma picked up in the kitchen, "Hello," in her normal sweet caring voice, she answered. The voice as she described—that of a course sounding white man, informed, "You Niggers getting out your place—we will kill everyone of you and those Nigger lovers from the North— damn you!" Momma hung up the phone and completed dinner. After everyone was seated around the table and wherever they could sit in the dining room, she calmly walked in and said, "Got a call tonight. There are some people who want to hurt you." "Hurt us?" David questioned. "Yes, but it's going to be all right—as long as we know He (she pointed up) is on our side." Almost simultaneously, we began to sing to the top of our voices, "We shall overcome! We shall overcome! We shall overcome someday! Deep in my heart, I do believe, we shall overcome someday!"

Within a few days, David began setting up office for the Vicksburg *Citizen's Appeal* and a Library at the freedom school building. Working late into the night, he stayed over in the building, sleeping on a cot. He had solicited books and journals from a number of sources. The new library was almost filled with books and, by now, the *Citizen's Appeal* had successfully distributed its fifth bi-weekly edition. We were all quite proud of the accomplishments, particularly the fact that the freedom school had opened and had 25 eager black students.

During the first week of August, 1963, David came over to our house as usual for dinner and relaxation with his "southern family." As he prepared to leave, Momma stopped him at the front door and said, "Wait David, I don't want you to stay at that freedom school tonight. Rather have you stay here with me. I'm going to make a pound cake later tonight. You stay here." Without questioning, David turned and accepted her offer.

Little did any of us know how prophetic Momma's insistence on David's remaining at our house was that night. Somewhere after 2 a.m. our telephone rang. Daddy answered and the voice on the other end said, "Nigger, we have blown that building to hell!" We immediately rushed to our freedom school and found it literally blown to pieces, in smoldering ashes and sporadic fires that popped up here and there.

I shall never forget the look on Daddy's face as he got out of his 1947 Ford truck and painfully uttered ... "Lord have mercy on their souls!"

THE ROADS ARE DEFINED

The bombing of the Baptist Academy—our freedom school—only made us more determined and sealed our efforts for racial equality. That evening at the house, Daddy and Momma asked Jessie Lee, the Civil Rights workers, and me to come into the living room. There was a fire that burned in Daddy's eyes, and I was quite positive it glowed of the fire burning deep in his heart. "Let me tell y'all something," Daddy began to lecture. "Right is right and wrong is wrong. I know what we are trying to do here is right. Nobody can change that...they may not like it...I have four sons who are right now fighting for this country. Edward Lee left here because he was tired of being in the bottom—I don't mean the place where we stay here—but the bottom of this society. We may never leave this place (the Bottom), but we sure can do all we can to get up on the top," he continued. Momma's gentle voice intervened, "The best way to make it from the Bottom is to stick together. "Charles bring me the broom." I obeyed her request, confused, as I had no idea how the broom would fit into the discussion. Momma pulled some straws from the broom, and handed one of them to me. "Now, break it," she said as she looked on compassionately. Without effort, I broke the straw as all eyes watched carefully. Momma then gave me a handful of straws she had bundled together and said, "Now break them." I tried desperately, but was unsuccessful. With great satisfaction, Momma said, "Life is like the straws of this broom. Pull one out, you can break it, but if all the straws stick together, you can't—remember that for the rest of your life." Momma took a seat and sat quietly as Daddy completed the lesson. He looked at David and the other freedom fighters and said, "You have come here to show us Negroes the way in Mississippi. I thank you. All my life I have been on the short end of the stick, working long with Rosa to raise my children and teach them to respect themselves and others. One day, all of them will be gone from this Bottom and we have told them that the roads from the bottom are:

1. Know yourself

2. Respect yourself and others
3. Have faith
4. Get a good education
5. Never give up
6. Associate with people who are trying to advance
7. Help somebody else
8. Stand up for something
9. Trust in God
10. Pray daily

"They bombed that building up there, but they can't bomb what we know to be right out of us." Tears welled in our eyes as Momma began to sing: "Amazing grace, how sweet the sound, that saved a wretch like me; I once was lost, but now, I'm found, was blind, but now I see." We all joined in the next verse, proclaiming as of the recent bombing, "Through many dangers, toils and snares, I have already come. 'Twas grace that brought me safe thus far, and grace will lead me home."

Certainly, it was God's grace and protective hand that had given Momma the foresight to insist that David remain at our house the night before. Without question, David would have died in the explosion, for the cot where he would have slept that night was never found.

14

The Piano Player Won't Play

In 1963, during the time Daddy was out of work and was struggling to run his own glass shop, I took a job at Tuminellos' Restaurant down near the railroad track. My nephew, Junior, had told one of the owners that I could play the piano and organ at the same time, and she hired me to provide music Thursday through Saturday nights. Since I was just in the 9th grade, $10 per night was a large salary. Even larger were the tips that amounted to no less than $50 on slow nights and near $90 when the crowds were large. I was rolling in money, bringing home no less than $60, three nights each week.

Wealthy, good-tipping customers requested a wide range of old tunes—including *Hello Dolly*, *Misty*, *Canadian Sunset*, *Misty Blue*, *Unchained Melody*, *St. Louis Blues*, *Tennessee Waltz*, *Indian Love Song* and on and on. God had blessed me with the gift of music and perfect recall. I loved it when the customers would sing with the music. Their singing was always louder and more rambunctious as the night grew older and their empty cocktail glasses mounted on the tables.

In addition to salary and tips, I was allowed to have my choice from the menu at break time. Don't know why I always wanted the same thing—a big hamburger and french fries. The black people who worked in the kitchen were all very nice, and often I played their requests as they stood with ear to door, sneaking a quick moment of rest. The head chef, an elderly, kind black man always said, "When you go back in there, play my song." His song—*Blue Moon*.

Ole Miss had a big football game over at Memorial Stadium in Jackson, Mississippi one night. The town of Vicksburg had buzzed with "Rebels" all day, honking car

88

Charles at high school graduation, 1966.

horns and waving Confederate flags. Tuminello's was the gathering spot for reveling Rebels after football games. This night was no exception. About 11:00, the crowd had thickened to capacity. There was much singing..."Twenty two bottles of beer on the wall, twenty two bottles of beer; if one of the bottles should slip and fall there's twenty one bottles of beer..." One wiped-out, teary-eyed white lady came over to the piano, put $10 in my jar and said, "Boy, play *Danny Boy*." I did. She cried from "The pipes, the pipes are calling" to "the summer's gone." By the time I made it to "But come ye back," she lay sprawled out on the floor. I was not sure whether she fainted or had a blackout. Didn't matter, she had paid her $10.

Many other request were made, and I obliged. A stout, red-faced white man staggered over to the piano, sat on the end of the keyboard, causing a most unmelodic sound, and said, "Hey boy—play *Dixie*!" I slowly looked around at him and responded, "I'll play *Dixie*, if you help me sing *We Shall Overcome.*" He seemed to sober up and jumped up from his comfortable seat on the keys, allowing me to play the keys his rear end had covered and yelled, "You say what, boy?!" Without thought or fear I repeated, "I'll play *Dixie* if you help me sing *We Shall Overcome.*" He rushed away from the piano like a mad animal. I knew I was in deep trouble, but I didn't care. Quick thoughts of what the reference to *Dixie* meant to black people rushed through my mind. It was the symbol of white hostility towards blacks and denoted the wishes of many southerners to remain in a position of superiority over the black man. It was a southern anthem of racism. It was not going to be played—at least not by me! Not that night, nor any other night. Within minutes, one of the managers walked over to me and questioned, "Charlie, did you refuse to play *Dixie*?!" "Yes," I responded. "I'm awfully sorry, but you'll have to leave!" she said angrily as she strutted away.

As I walked home after midnight, I thought about what had happened. I thought about the money that was coming in handy. Daddy's comments about roads from bottom places came clearly to mind: "Always respect yourself." I knew that the *Dixie* request was made mostly as an insult. I continued to ponder the lyrics of the song..."I wish I was in the land of cotton; old times there are not forgotten; look away, look away, look away Dixieland." I had gone to the cotton field once in my life and had seen feeble, old black men and women working alongside youthful blacks in the field, from sunup to sundown, for $3. I was reminded of slavery in Dixie—the South. I well understood the sentiments of the song's author who made reference to the "old times in the South" not being forgotten. Old times — Jim Crow, Black Codes, slavery, lynchings. Perhaps when he thought of Dixie his heart was endeared; when I thought of Dixie, my heart was broken.

I did not bother to awaken my parents when I made it home. The next morning, as we were getting ready for Sunday school, I told Momma and Daddy that I had been fired and why. Daddy said, "I am proud of you. Don't ever let anybody force you to do things that you know are not right. God gave you the gift of music. Don't play any song unless you can play it from your heart." From that day to this one, I have remembered his instructions. When I play, I play from my heart.

WA JU'S STORE

It was at the end of the school year, 1963. Daddy came home for lunch. For some reason Momma was there and not out at All Saints College where she worked as a cook. "Wa Ju wants to sell me the store, Rosa," he blurted as he ate. "Sell you the store? What you gonna do with a store? Who will run it?" Daddy did not answer her right then as her questions signaled her interest. Momma moved the dishes from the table and Daddy headed to the front door.

Wa Ju's store becomes Chip's Grocery—In the heart of Marcus Bottom.

"He only wants $10,000 and I can get Mr. Cox to stand for that." "Well talk about it when you come home." Daddy's mind was set—he would get the store—that's the way he did things — don't sit and wait too long—strike while the iron is hot.

Wa Ju's store was one of three Chinese-owned grocery stores in Marcus Bottom.. For years, Wa Ju, his wife, and three children had run the store on the corner of Bomar Avenue and Halls Ferry Road. Many black boys in the community, including my brothers Boo and Edward Lee, had held part-time delivery jobs at the store. They rode bicycles with sacks of groceries strapped in baskets. The store always smelled "Chinese" with the pervading aroma of garlic and other stuff Chinese people like to cook. Wa Ju had charge accounts and the loyalty of many black people in the community. I remember how many of us were confused and lost as Wa Ju and his family communicated in Chinese. It was funny. I was always sure they were talking about us.

At 5:30 that evening, Daddy came home. "Well, Rosa, what you think?" "I don't know, Chiplin," Momma replied. "Let's go down here and talk to Wa Ju," Daddy insisted. Moments later they walked down Smith Alley to the store.

After about an hour, Momma and Daddy returned. As Momma walked in, she said, "We are going to buy Wa Ju's store." I was so excited—just the thought of owning the grocery store meant a lot to me. Within several days, we went with our parents to look through the store, which included a two-story apartment in the rear.

Much talk arose in the Bottom when word was out about the store purchase. As Daddy and Wa Ju had closed their deal, Jessie, Momma, Daddy and I went down to learn the basic operations. We had to learn fast because the store was to continue operations the next day under new management.

Wa Ju acquainted us with his credit system: a wooden box with brown books bearing the accounts of numerous blacks in the community. Daddy agreed to continue the credit business—after all, that was the survival of neighborhood grocery stores.

The next day came—Saturday morning. Daddy called out through the house, "Rise and shine!" This was 6 a.m. on Saturday morning. The cartoons hadn't even come on T.V. We knew to get up immediately, for Daddy was a stickler for promptness, always reminding, "The early bird gets the worm!" "Who wants a worm anyway?" I always wondered in my sometimes rebellious spirit.

First-day business operations were not unusual. Wa Ju stood around to assist if needed. The clapping of a cowbell against the front door signaled the entrance of customers, black folks from Marcus Bottom. The business became pretty brisk as more and more folks came to see the "black Chinese" running the store. Most people were genuinely happy of the change and wished us well.

The first night, some black guys stood around outside and made comments that last even to now. "Can't no black man run no grocery store and make a living!" "It's too many of them Chiplins in there; they won't stay in business a good month!" ...(laugh) "Nigga Chinamons!" These and other comments didn't alter my father's determination, which by now had gripped all of us. We trusted his judgment. We had seen him struggle before and make it—why should this be any different? We had seen him build a freedom school literally with nothing and make an extensive addition to the side of our shotgun house, also with limited resources.

Daddy was offered his former job at the glass company, and Momma assumed the major responsibility of store operations. She was a phenomenal businessperson, adored throughout the community and loved cash customers, credit customers and those who stopped by for a handout. She had a way with route salesmen who were willing to extend a range of stock on credit. They never had to worry about their money. They looked forward to stopping at Chip's Grocery where the kind, witty, but firm black lady would greet them, insist on their drinking coffee with her or trying one of her many recipes she had cooked the night before.

We often jokingly remarked, "Momma gives away more

food than she sells across the counter." That didn't stop her, because she firmly believed and lived to see it over and over again: "Freely you give, freely shall you receive."

The extent of the credit business grew even larger. Most customers charged groceries throughout the month and settled up at payday or when social assistance checks arrived. Every now and then there were exceptions—people charged at Chips and walked on the other side of the street to avoid my mother and father on paydays.

Chip's Grocery became a community gathering place for Mr. Troy, Booney Hall, Miss Baby, Miss Ceasar and numerous others. They came not only for grocery purchases, but to share conversations—to laugh, to cry, to find out, to tell.

It was a kinder and gentler time in most Southern communities, and particularly in Marcus Bottom. Momma and Daddy closed the store most nights about 10:00 and drove home. There was no apparent need for security guards to ensure their safety. Money from the day's business operations was stuffed into a paper bag which was, on one occasion, left on the top of the car as they drove home. Many nights, they slept in the front room with the window raised and the money bag under the bed. Daddy had a pistol that he never fired except on New Year's Eve after church services up at Mt. Carmel, and an old shotgun that stood in the corner by the bed. He only used it for rabbit hunting in season. Thoughts of defense from violent attacks were far removed—besides who was going to harm the people who befriended them?

Life for blacks in the Bottom remained quiet and "easy like Sunday morning." People worked during the week, white women drove nice cars with their dogs seated up front to pick up their black maids and cooks or yardmen, who rode on the back seat. The same pride with which these devoted employees cleaned white homes, tended white children, cooked meals for white families, and manicured white folks yards was equally exemplified around their own houses down in Marcus Bottom. Most were always "health department" clean, with small yards outside smelling of and radiant with brightly colored flowers, particularly roses.

Traffic grew pretty heavy around 5:30 in the afternoon, as people returned home from work or drove through enroute to places beyond the Bottom.

By 7:00 p.m., usually everything was settled. People, during the warmer months, sat out on their front porches—screened or not—it didn't matter. Most people did not have air conditioners. Even those few who did elected to sit outside for the mere sake of visiting with neighbors and watching what happened—very little—the loudest noises came from either of several cafes—The Melody Lounge, Jessie Singleton's place and Deliah's Dew Drop Inn. Of course, there were those who drank, liked to dance and shot pool in back rooms of the cafes. Rumor always had it that they rolled dice too. Amidst even those "evils," rarely were there reports of fights.

15

This Little Light of Mine

The *Citizen's Appeal* continued to gain support in Vicksburg as did the Civil Rights movement. More and more, people began to talk of change and were rapidly becoming aware of just how far behind (in terms of racial equality) Mississippi and most assuredly, Vicksburg, was. The work and dedication of the freedom workers had ignited a fire that burned of our want for freedom, causing us to sing: "I'm on my way to freedom land; I'm on my way to freedom land; I'm on my way to freedom land; I'm on my way—Thank God, I'm on my way."

Just before the summer of 1964, Dr. and Mrs. Aaron Shirley told us that they were going to drive to Atlantic City, New Jersey to participate in efforts of the newly formed Mississippi Freedom Democratic Party (MFDP). The MFDP planned an attempt to unseat the regular State Democratic Party at its National Convention. It was all very exciting. Mrs. Ollie Shirley, who had inspired and taught me in the seventh grade, asked if I wanted to go with them. OF COURSE! I don't remember sleeping too soundly for at least two weeks leading up to our departure.

Throughout Mississippi, the Freedom Democratic Party, headed by Dr. Aaron Henry, was inspired tremendously through the efforts of Fannie Lou Hamer and had held local caucuses and selected delegates—brave black men and women with courage to even envision such a mammoth undertaking. It would be quite a challenge. Black people from the then, and now, near poorest state in the nation, a state sweltering with blatant acts of racial hostility, would at last be heard in a national forum. Buses were chartered across the state and people, having packed for the long trip to Atlantic City, boarded with their luggage, boarded with their burning desire to be heard, if not counted. Dr. Shirley, his family (sons — Terry and Kevin, daughter—Crystal and his wife) and I packed our luggage in his Rambler station wagon and began the long journey. Not having traveled too far away from Vicksburg before, the trip to me was like a journey around the world.

I thought the farther away from Mississippi we traveled, the farther away from racial prejudice and discrimination we were. I was wrong. We were allowed entrance at a number of restaurants and other quick stops along the way, but the stares we received from white patrons and business owners reminded me of those back home. Dr. Shirley pointed out that blacks were treated as second-class citizens all over this nation and that racism in other parts of the country, though much subtle, was just as strong and dangerous as southern racism.

At last, we were there—Atlantic City, New Jersey—the Board Walk—people basking in the sun—music in the air—..."under the boardwalk, under the boardwalk, on a blanket with my baby, that's where I'll be." The Mississippi Freedom Democratic Party delegates had no time to "be under the boardwalk;" rather there was much serious planning and negotiating to be done.

We checked into our hotel. Dr. Shirley left almost immediately for a scheduled strategy session. Later that evening, he came back and carried us to a mass rally for the MFDP at a nearby church. I had seen Mrs. Fannie Lou Hamer on T.V. and listened as she shared her story of her brutal attack in jail by several men who were forced to beat her up simply because she and some others in their Delta town of Ruleville, Mississippi had tried to register to vote. And now, I sat at the organ, playing for this thunderous black woman as she sang: "This little light of mine, I'm gonna let it shine...Jesus give it to me, I'm gonna let it shine." Following her song, she spoke and her last words stuck with me...."I'm just sick and tired of being sick and tired." There's something about the way she said it, something about the way she looked, with her left eye nearly closed from stress. Much to our surprise, we received a

97

visit from Dr. Ralph Abernathy and Rev. Dr. Martin Luther King. There I was, a 16 year old boy from Marcus Bottom, playing the organ as King led us in singing: "We shall overcome, we shall overcome, we shall overcome some day; deep in my heart, I do believe, we shall overcome some day."

While the Mississippi Freedom Democratic Party was not successful in unseating the regular state party, its impact was tremendous, bringing national and international attention to a number of racial injustices in Mississippi. As a token of consolation, the MFDP was given two seats at large on the floor of the convention, though with no vote.

Following the convention, we returned to Vicksburg with an even greater zeal for freedom and justice. One thing was certain: our fires had been rekindled and ours was a deeper commitment to "Let our lights shine!"

AN UNDECLARED WAR

Many of the freedom workers went home after the summer of 1964. Most returned to college. Whites in Vicksburg who were most verbally opposed to the freedom movement and other whites assumed that with the "troublemakers," "outside agitators" gone, they could return to their normal separatist practices and activities. They were wrong. Black perspective had largely changed, and freedom efforts continued. Some of us went to the Joy Theater which for many years had a separate "crow's nest" seating area for black upstairs and white, plush seating for whites downstairs. We were refused admittance downstairs, but kept going back.

Freedom riders came through Vicksburg—black and white college students who rode the Greyhound and Trailways buses (sitting up front) across the South, staging sit-ins at restaurants that were for whites only. They sat-in at restaurants in downtown Vicksburg and were intimidated.

Daddy was still determined to have freedom classes, and I took on the assignment of teaching neighborhood children and my nieces and nephews on the back porch of our house. Back porch school was serious business. The students declare that their real formal education came sitting on the back porch and down the back stairs of our house. I had read the *World Book Encyclopedia* from A to Z by this time and had also read through most of the black history books we had salvaged from the freedom school building. Linda, my sister's oldest daughter, now a pediatrician in Jackson, Mississippi, recalls: "Uncle Charles was so mean and strict. He made us study and learn when the other children were out playing hide-and-go-seek."

The freedom movement was off limits to most black churches in Vicksburg and many black ministers not only refused to actively participate but joined white inspired efforts to put an end to the struggle.

New Mt. Pilgrim, Shiloh, Wesley United Methodist, Pleasant Green M. B. Church and Grove Street M. B. Church were among the few black churches allowing for freedom forums and mass meetings initially. Daddy was insistent upon our family church, Mt. Carmel, allowing freedom meetings. Finally, after prevailing over the objections of a few members, Mt. Carmel also joined the network of "freedom churches."

By the beginning of 1964, a number of black ministers were active in the movement, preaching sermons at mass meetings and standing with protesters throughout the city. Reverends O. H. Hunter, T. H. Turner, Mayfield and Hosea Phillips were among the most verbal. Rev. Turner was a favorite mass meeting speaker. In the heated furor of his freedom messages, he would scratch his shining bald head, shout "Aw shucks!," and demonstrate how he had stood up to various persons who adamantly opposed equality for blacks.

A large number of stout-hearted black people were regulars at all meetings, and were counted on for services inclusive of telephone calling, making protest posters, picketting outside city administrative offices and preparing food. Momma and Daddy, Lee Willa Miller, Mildred (Topsey) Cosey, Mary Carter, Pink Taylor, Mary Smith, Mr. and Mrs. Charlie Hunt, Mrs. Hunter, Mr. and Mrs. William

Tripplet, Frank Crump, Frank Summers, and Mr. and Mrs. Charlie Phelps are some of the people who come readily to mind as they braved threats and intimidation for their stand.

The movement grew even stronger in Vicksburg as we were visited by National spokesmen for the Southern Christian Leadership Conference (SCLC), National Association for the Advancement of Colored People (NAACP), Student Non-Violent Coordinating Committee (SNCC) and others. My mother received a telephone call early one morning in 1965 from a lady who had lived for a while in the Old Baptist Academy Building. She told her that her daughter, 12 of age, had been raped by a white man the night before, and that he paid $50 and was released from jail. Outraged, my mother began to call people and by night, the biggest mass meeting ever was held. Many angry, thunderous voices were heard that night and I distinctly remember Daddy standing and saying, "We have sat by and allowed a lot of wrong things to happen in this city. They (the whites) take us for granted! And now, they rape one of our daughters, pay a $50 fine, and go on about their life! If we will strike, we must strike while the iron is hot, and believe me fellow Christians, it is sure enough hot!"

Within a few days, blacks had organized a selective buying campaign (boycott) against white-owned stores, with the exception of a few whose owners pledged support. Ours and several other black grocery stores began to feel the impact of increased black business.

At last, black people were patronizing black business on a much larger scale—much the same as other minority groups in America had done for many years. Increased profits for black business owners made it possible for them to hire additional help and lower prices—a common economic rule. Black businesses made much needed contributions to the freedom movement.

My father, as a leader of the movement, was singled out for attack and intimidation from the white community. I wondered why was there so much alarm about black people uniting and supporting each other. It was evident that whites had boycotted black businesses eternally. What was

100

so different about this? Then flashbacks of the colored water fountain, Buckwheat, and Jake Wagoner were imminent in my mind. The historical slave mentality had a dual effect: it kept former slaves feeling like slaves and former slaveowners feeling like slaveowners, even to that time, 100 years later. To stay focused, often in my heart there was a recurring melody, "And before I be a slave, I'll be buried in my grave and go home to my Lord and be free."

White business owners hardest hit by the boycott began to cry out, and requested several meetings with movement leaders. When requested to make statements reflecting their support for freedom efforts, and to hire blacks in management positions in their stores, their response was negative. They pointed out that whites would not trade with them if they actively supported and hired blacks.

The boycott grew increasingly stronger, as did tension in Vicksburg. As Momma attempted to cross Halls Ferry Road, walking to work during the fifth week of the boycott, a white man tried to run over her in his car. He had waited, with his motor idling, until she was midway the street. A black boy standing in front of Chip's Grocery yelled to her, "Miss Chiplin, watch out!" Dropping her purse and running, she narrowly escaped the attempt on her life. I shudder even to think of what might have happened if my mother had been killed. Momma's spirit was heightened. That's the way she was. Nothing or nobody could ever get her down—she had, as a very young lady, thrown an ax and killed a bull that was attacking my brothers, T. J. and Edward Lee, back down on Wagoner's Plantation. With courage to spare, she rallied even greater support for freedom efforts in Vicksburg.

Leading up to the Fourth Sunday in November, 1965, we started receiving threatening phone calls, both at the store and at home. Several teachers at Rosa A. Temple High School and the principal called me and my sister Jessie into the office and told us that if we didn't stop participating in the "Civil Rights stuff," we would be expelled from school. Daddy commented that the educators no doubt had been forced to tell us that and no matter what, we would continue to work.

The threatening telephone calls became more frequent and hostile. "Hello?" "Watch the damn fire!...Slam!" "Was that another prank call?" Momma asked as she cut meat on the chopping block in the store. "I reckon so," Daddy answered from behind the counter. Beyond the intimidating calls, it was a usual Sunday night run of business at Chip's. Mr. Troy in his usual slow manner, filled the drink boxes. Miss Ceasar sipped a brew, taking in any and all conversations. Booney Hall (our cousin) joked with Momma. Guys stood around outside the store. The night was, from all appearances, normal.

Daddy flipped the sign to "closed" on the front door around 10 p.m. and went outside to lock the kerosene tank. Momma counted the money and put it into a paper bag while I straightened some stock on the shelves. By now, Jessie was away in school at Tennessee State University.

Boo (James, Jr.), his wife, Bertha, and two children, Annette and Anthony Troy went upstairs in the apartment adjoining the store. By 10:30, Momma, Daddy and I had made it home. Tired from the brisk business day, Daddy and Momma turned the T.V. on in their room and went to bed. By 11:00, I had retired to bed. The night remained normal. At 11:30, we were thrown from our beds. There was an enormously loud noise that deafened our ears and sounded like a combination of thunder, an atomic explosion, and the upheaval of the world at judgment day. Screams penetrated the darkness which was caused by a broken power line in the community. Mrs. Maggie Gibson's voice was raised over the screams as she cried out, "Mr. Chiplin, your store is on fire!!"

We ran to the end of Smith's Alley and saw the ruins of the undeclared war. The store and apartment where my brother and family lived was in shambles and flames and there were explosions that pierced the ears and our hearts.

Daddy and Momma ran on towards the store. I ran back to the house and pulled Daddy's 45 revolver from under the bed and jumped into the 1964 Chevrolet. As I was backing into the Alley, Mrs. Josie Ennon came running, called out, "Charles! Wait!" She ran up to the car and asked where I

102

was going. I felt that whoever had bombed the store was watching from the top of a hill overlooking Marcus Bottom. I was going to kill them. Mrs. Ennon, with tears streaming down, said, "Charles, please don't go get yourself in trouble....the Lord watching all of this—vengeance is His!" "And mine!" I abruptly shouted. Mrs. Ennon stood behind the car, prohibiting me to back out. Realizing that she was acting out of love, I got out of the car, still gripping the gun, and ran to join the scores of others at the store who looked on in disbelief.

There is a God. We saw His miraculous workings that night in Marcus Bottom at Chip's Grocery. We saw two babies thrown from upstairs through fire and not burned. We saw my brother and wife unscratched although the bed they had slept in was blown away. We saw fire engulf the kerosene tank and it did not explode. What more did we need to see?

As firefighters tried to put out the series of fires, someone in the crowd led off singing, "We shall overcome, we shall overcome, we shall overcome some day." I knew then, if not any point before, people in Marcus Bottom had experienced an awakening and were ready to stand up for what was right.

The impact of the bombing was felt for miles away. Up to 10 blocks in each direction, people's windows, roofs, and bathroom appliances were cracked. A white policeman walked over to my father and said, "Your store was bombed with dynamite. There is a hole deep and wide as a house at the side of the building." A closer examination revealed that the attackers had left a junk car on the side of the store earlier, loaded it with dynamite and timed it to go off at 9:00 p.m. Fortunately, the timer did not function as planned. Many lives perhaps would have been lost had it worked. Once more we were reminded of Divine Providence.

After about three hours of rallying and singing at the wrecked building, people returned home. Early the next morning, lines of cars filed past the demolished building. People came from everywhere to see the "remains of war."

My father, the brave, stout-hearted man that he was, proudly walked down Smith Alley and down to the store the next morning on time—7 a.m., stood in the middle of the rubble and announced to the top of his voice, "I am open for business!"

Somehow, business did continue. People traded at the makeshift counter Daddy set up. He sold those things that were salvageable. Momma called on her vendors, who readily came and brought additional stock. Neighbors pitched in to help rebuild the building.

My brother (Buddy) Alfred, Sr., was at the same time fighting for this country in Vietnam. From his foxhole, he wrote a letter to the President of the United States which in effect read: "I am in Vietnam, fighting for the cause of democracy. At home in Vicksburg, Mississippi, my family has been attacked because they also believe in freedom and democracy for everybody."

Ebony and *Jet* magazines came to Vicksburg and covered the story. The publicity was all right, but more important was the resolution of the issues that had caused the boycott. For nearly a month, the boycott continued. Finally, a group of white business owners met, seriously made an appeal to city hall, and pledged to correct a number of racist policies and practices. The boycott was lifted.

16

Riding Up Front—Living in the Back

Life would never be the same in Vicksburg, particularly in Marcus Bottom. A new sense of black pride and determination surfaced. Those loyal maids and yardmen who had previously ridden on the back seats of their employers' cars now rode up front or drove their own cars to work. Salaries for black workers, although not commensurate with those of whites, increased. Blacks had been hired on the police department. They were not given cars, walked to patrol their beats, and had to call for the assistance of white officers when arresting a white person. Even still, this was better than having no blacks on the force.

Our household changed a little as Kenneth Ray, my brother Ray's son, came to live permanently with us. He had visited several times during summers and returned home. Daddy and Momma were concerned and loved him very much. His mother had 11 other children, and life for them was hard back down in Fayette. Kenneth's arrival signaled a return to basic parenting—P.T.A. meetings, homework assistance, and the like. He was just going to the eighth grade. With Jessie off in school at Tennessee State and me scheduled to leave for Tougaloo College, we were relieved and grateful that Kenneth would be there to help and be helped by our parents. We did not think of him as a nephew, but rather another brother. My parents considered all of their 38 grandchildren as their own children, and in return was respected as Momma and Daddy by all of them.

I spent one semester at Tougaloo College and transferred to Alcorn College at Lorman in order to drive home each evening and help in the store.

The late 1960s were marked by sporadic racial crisis in

As late as the '70s, some blacks in Vicksburg rode the back seat of their white employer's cars to work.

the South. "Freedom Summers" and other organized efforts were mounted to land the final blows at the shaken towering wall of racial prejudice and hate.

For the cause of freedom, much had happened in the South, and many lives had been lost. Medgar Evers, Field Secretary for the NAACP, had been slain in his driveway in Jackson, Mississippi by Byron de la Beckwith, a diehard segregationist. Beckwith was freed by two hung juries—white men and women who had little or no regard for justice. Three little black girls had been killed when their church was bombed during Sunday School in Little Rock, Arkansas; three Civil Rights workers had been brutally murdered in Philadelphia, Mississippi, and Rev. Dr. Martin L. King had been killed by James Earl Ray as he stood on a hotel balcony in Memphis, Tennessee, April 4, 1968.

The Vietnam War remained at the heart of national unrest. Certainly, racism was acutely prevalent and pronounced, as scores of black young men just turning 18 were drafted and immediately sent, after inadequate training, to the heat of battle. Many black mothers and fathers across the nation wept at gravesides of their young sons. This sorrow was deeply felt also in Vicksburg. The city's local draft board, headed by a white lady, Mrs. Wooten, had systematically selected and sentenced many of our classmates to die in Vietnam, "For the cause of democracy." One of the Bottom neighbors—Mr. and Mrs. Sherman Bracey, had pleaded desperately to have their son, Sherman reclassified, as he was the only son. Their pleas fell on the deaf ears of the local board that insisted he report for active duty. Within three months, Sherman Bracey was funeralized in the Bottom.

At nearby Jackson State College, racial tension exploded into a riot in May of 1970. Black college students, long disgruntled over the Vietnam War and over unfair, unequal, and unjust treatment by the City of Jackson and State College Board, took their protest to the street. Fueled by racial intimidations and slurs from white motorists who drove through the campus on Lynch Street, they endeavored to close the street. Traffic on Lynch Street additionally had been a barrier to their crossing to classes on the other side of the campus. Their protest spanned several days, and ended with a showdown with city police and the Mississippi National Guard. Two young black men—James Green and Phillip Gibbs—were killed in a barrage of barbaric fire.

Down south of Vicksburg at Alcorn where I was now a senior, there was also campus unrest, although no one was killed. My colleagues protested the strong hand of racial control held by then-President J. D. Boyd. Dormitories were set on fire, T.V. sets were thrown from upper story windows, and demonstrations were held, particularly at President Boyd's office. Alcornites were equally enraged with the Vietnam War.

Upon my graduation from Alcorn, as I accepted a teaching position at Jefferson Jr. High School in Vicksburg, the local Military Draft Board changed my draft status to 1-A and ordered me to show up for a physical. I passed and was soon to be sworn in. I was not going to Vietnam, even if it meant suffering the penalty of incarceration. We had survived one war in Marcus Bottom. There was absolutely no patriotic endearment in my heart at that time. Daddy told me to write and tell them how I felt. My letter to the local board read: "My country 'tis of thee, but where is the liberty of which I sing? I shall not die in war for the land wherein my fathers have died and been denied. I will not fire a single shot for this racist country." I often hummed a then popular song—"War! What is it good for—absolutely nothing!"

Perhaps they ruled me crazy or something, but they changed my draft status to 1-Y (whatever that was). I didn't have to go.

Our efforts with the Vicksburg battles continued. Others joined the fight: Thelma Rush, who had returned home to work at the Waterways Experiment Station, Robert Major Walker, an associate professor at Jackson State University, Michael and Larry Sims, schoolmates from Rosa A. Temple, and many others.

In 1971, we realized that many roads from the Bottom were still marked with racist signs. To some extent we had "overcome" a few things, but we had many more challenges ahead. Black students still received a separate and "unequal" education at Rosa A. Temple. White students gained from many educational advantages at Cooper High School. Streets in most black neighborhoods remained substandard. Black neighborhoods were flooded by each hard rain due to poor or non-existent drainage systems. No blacks were employed in managerial positions at major city businesses and industries. Strange, unresolved, and poorly investigated murders of black people were common. Promises of the white men who had earlier mediated to end the first boycott were generally unkept.

Near the summer of 1971, Rev. Eddie McBride, a black, militant former resident of Vicksburg, returned to assist in our efforts. Meeting with opposition from some blacks who wanted a much slower change, McBride organized the Concerned Citizens of Vicksburg with me as his co-chairman. Our protest included the previous issues with particular emphasis on the lopsided school system.

Immediately, the Vicksburg Concerned Citizens' freedom fight met with opposition, this time head-on from a group of black ministers who no doubt were prompted by local whites. The ministers pointed out in an early meeting that "a lot of changes had already been made in Vicksburg and there was no need to make people (white people) angry with us." Further, they accused Rev. McBride of being a trouble-maker, and labeled Jim Chiplin (my father) a threat to the community. This labeling grew out of his freedom struggles that had led to the bombings of two buildings. For all practical purposes—all of the Chiplins, especially me, were written off as "hot headed" by blacks who were content with things as they were and whites who were bent on keeping them that way.

With heated opposition from some black preachers, Daddy called a meeting of deacons from local churches. About 20 showed up at Grove Street Church where they organized the Vicksburg Deacon's Alliance with Daddy as President. Included among the purposes of the Alliance were: 1) assisting the freedom movement in Vicksburg; 2) helping to make churches aware of racial injustices and available for meeting purposes; 3) fulfilling biblical instructions for deacons—attending to the business of the church, assisting the spirituality of the church and coming to the aid of widows and orphans. The Alliance was not recognized, nor accepted for the previous purposes, but was labeled rather as "Mr. Chiplin's trouble-making deacons." As a result, Charlie Hunt, Charlie Steele, James Brown, Eunice Brown, Harry Powell and the ladies who joined the Alliance—

Mildred Cosey, Rosa Chiplin, Mrs. Hunt, Mrs. Hunter—were all "trouble-makers."

In an early address to the Deacon's Alliance, Daddy said:

> The deacon's place in the spread of the Gospel came through a cry made by the Grecians against the Hebrews that their widows were neglected in the daily ministration of the ministers...Those ministers, the 12, called the multitude together to work out a plan for the distribution of such as they had for the satisfaction of the suffering people who were being neglected....seven men whom they knew and considered to be worthy and well qualified were recommended for the task of deacons....
>
> The deacon's duty is to see to the welfare of the church; to see that the rules and regulations of the body are properly adhered to....It is incumbent upon each officer of the church to see that every sheep of the fold has the same provisions. We are not to make flesh of some and bones of others. When the church does not rise to its proper responsibility in the community it serves, it is opening the door for its members to go and scratch in the trash piles for the necessities of their survival...The only thing our churches want to keep going is a 'church society'...All other races seem to care much more about their people than us...The love for one another should be 'the tie that binds' us in Christianity... I'm mighty afraid that it would be hard to get someone to preach in our churches, if no money came up in the offering.

Many of Daddy's references were from the country—back down in Jefferson County. His was the spirit of the country—sharing what little you had—neighbors looking out for each other—"helping to pick out each others rows," "making the mule plow."

Continuing, he said... "America would not need a welfare system, if we were true to our call as Christians....If we brought our tithes into the storehouse and used them for the sacred purposes they were intended, we could meet the needs of the poor that we have with us always." His pleadings were heard and accepted by his fellow deacons from various Vicksburg churches but viewed with disdain by many of the preachers. Nevertheless, they would become the axle of the wheel of the Vicksburg Freedom Fight.

Rev. McBride and I continued to meet with people across

town, making them aware of our present situation—still not nearly where we as blacks should be in terms of equality. Having prepared a list of concerns for the black community, we assembled a committee of Blacks to meet at City Hall and invited a number of white businessmen. Travis Vance, Sr. was Mayor of Vicksburg. He, a shrewd politician, agreed to meet and listened attentively to our concerns, which were to: 1) upgrade blacks on the police department immediately; 2) hire blacks on the fire department; 3) immediately improve drainage in black communities; 4) improve streets in black communities; 5) hire blacks at City Hall immediately; and 6) use the influence of city administration to encourage the employment of blacks in managerial positions at local businesses. The meeting ended with a verbal agreement by the mayor to immediately "set the wheels in motion" to meet our request. Weeks passed—nothing happened—absolutely nothing.

We called the first large meeting of the Concerned Citizens Movement at Grove Street Church. People showed up in mass numbers. There was much singing and rhetoric and a resolution to initiate once again a selective buying campaign against white merchants until our demands to the city were met.

A team of poster-makers stayed on after the meeting and worked late into the night, hurriedly writing protest signs that read: "Freedom Now!" "Blacks—Last Hired—First Fired!" "End Slavery In Vicksburg!" etc. By 9:00 the next morning, picketers were all across the city, sharing our message with potential customers at a number of businesses. It did not take much convincing to get most black people to honor the boycott, as Vicksburg's racial injustices were by now a sore issue with many.

The most feared of the protestors was an elderly, muscular black man called "Bouncer" (Albert Johnson). He had lived and worked hard in Vicksburg for many years and, unlike many people his age, was not afraid. In fact, we had to keep a close eye on him to ensure that he didn't rough anybody up.

As I drove onto the parking lot of Humpty Dumpty Grocery Store on Openwood Street around 6:00 one afternoon, I noticed a large crowd of people tiptoeing to see something at the center of the crowd. Jumping out of the car, I ran into the crowd only to find Bouncer literally holding a frail black man in the air by his collar. I yelled, "Bouncer, put him down!" as the crowd roared with laughter. Putting him down was not at the top of Bouncer's immediate concerns. He questioned, "Who is this funny looking fellah? Told me he go in any store he want to!" With that statement, Bouncer drew back to nail him one. Desperately, I prevailed, and Bouncer slowly let him down. I explained that the gentleman was Rev. Lanier. My introduction triggered Bouncers anger again as he swooped him up and said, "A preacher? I ought to really black your eyes!" Descending once more and at last free of Bouncer's massive hands, Rev. Lanier scurried away to the jeers of the crowd as he proclaimed, "It's a disgrace! These white folks ain't done nothing to us! All y'all going to hell!" While the episode appeared amusing to most, some of us were concerned that Rev. Lanier's remarks represented the convictions of many blacks, not only in Vicksburg, who had internalized racism as an acceptable state of being in the South.

To make it convenient for elderly blacks and others, we negotiated and left three major white supermarkets off the selective buying campaign. None to our surprise, a number of white stores—grocery, clothing, auto parts, etc., began to deliver to black customers who did not want to be seen breaking the boycott, once more signaling the importance of the black dollar.

The basic principles of business were being instilled in a number of neighborhood children. They were given a chance to work and earn money at Chip's Grocery. Johnnie's baby son Marcus was a carbon copy of his grandfather, and showed up early at the store each morning and waited at the door. Each morning, he was just as eager to work and looked up at Daddy and said, "Grandaddy, I'm ready to work, are you?" He worked hard and had an unusual ability to remember prices and customers' full names.

While driving on Openwood Street one morning, I saw a

For Sale sign on an abandoned grocery store. The store, a large old wood frame building with a house adjoining, had been operated some years earlier by two white ladies. After my loud knocks on the door, Mrs. Taylor, one of the owners, answered and informed that they wanted $15,000 for the property. My excitement mounted as I drove home, thinking of the possibilities for that place. It was located in a large old settled black community, a massive federal subdivision, Rolling Acres, had recently been completed down the hill. My excitement was tempered with cautions of what might be said of another store purchase, particularly during the boycott.

After sharing the information with Momma and Daddy, I listened as he gave his summation: "I have been wanting to expand the grocery business. That sounds like a good location. I know, however, that people will accuse us of taking advantage of this boycott." Momma interjected: "Chiplin, the boycotts don't last long. Pretty soon these people will be back to shopping at white stores as usual. If we can get the place, it would be good for the sake of our people and the little Chiplin grands."

By the next morning, we visited the Taylors and confirmed our intentions to purchase their property. Mrs. Taylor somehow felt strongly that we would and removed the For Sale sign.

Within two days, I wrote a business proposal for the Small Business Administration (SBA), submitted it and received the official loan application. Within two weeks, Momma called me in and said, "The loan was approved. They are letting us have $25,000." That amount, plus some personal savings, allowed us to open the second store on Openwood Street.

By now, the boycott was well into its seventh week and going strong. We saw little black children walking with picket signs holding on to their mothers' dress tails and elderly black men and women, bent from years of hard work, standing in front of City Hall, raising their voices singing: "I'm on my way to Freedom land, I'm on my way to Freedom land. I'm on my way to Freedom land, I'm on my way, thank God, I'm on my way!"

JAIL

The boycott continued into the summer of 1971. I had sought to continue teaching in Vicksburg, but was denied further employment because of my leadership role in the Civil Rights movement. Wanting to teach, I accepted a job at Oakley Training School as a music and math instructor. My involvement in the movement continued; in fact, it became more intense.

After returning from work at Oakley one afternoon, I got my picket sign and went with a group to a small shopping complex down Highway 61, south of Vicksburg. We had stood there for nearly an hour in the sweltering heat. A white policeman drove up. As he exited the patrol car, we were angered by his shouts: "Y'all Negras breaking the law, I'll put all your asses in jail!" This really was not a good time for him to harass the group. We were tired. Most of us had pulled eight hours on the job that day. It was hot. We were hot. He walked right up in my face and yelled, "Negra, your ass ain't got no business standing out here!" I replied, "Your ass ain't either!" He made a threatening advance and I drew back to hit him. I thought for sure he would shoot me. But it didn't matter right then. Several of the picketers pulled me back, explaining how serious the situation was. He rushed and put handcuffs on me and literally threw me in the car. All the way to the police station, he blurted how he should have shot me and that next time he would. I stood angry in the same police station where, as a boy I had stood, defying the segregated bus system. My brother Boo (James, Jr.) had been employed a couple of years earlier with the police department, and happened to be on the desk. He booked me on a charge of criminal conspiracy and turned around and released me on his recognizance bond. He better have. Within the hour, I was back down Highway 61 with a group led by Rev. McBride. I did not have time to tell McBride of the events that had led to my earlier arrest and within an hour, the entire group was arrested, booked on criminal conspiracy, and put in the Warren County Jail. Boo was not on duty. We were thrown into a cell with several drunks who reeked of rotgut whiskey. One had apparently been in a fight and was bloody. They refused to feed us that night. The night was longer than other nights, as the stench of the nasty cells prevailed and the extreme heat of the unventilated facility gripped and weakened us.

I was due at Oakley at 8:00 the next morning. Some others in our group were also scheduled for work. We couldn't go, but it didn't matter. We were in jail for a cause. We were "criminal conspirators"—whatever that meant. Daddy came up to the jail to inform me that he was raising a property bond of $25,000 to get me out. I told him not to worry and I was content to stay with the others. That afternoon around 4:00, Boo brought Momma up to the jail. She asked only one question, "Are you all all right?" We responded "Yes," and she began to sing at the top of her voice, "Some glad morning when this life is over, I'll fly away to a land where joy shall never end—I'll fly away!" Having completed several more verses, she turned to walk off, but stopped with tears in her eyes and said to me, "Remember the straws in the broom—stick together, they can't break us!"

We were all released on property bonds solicited by my father and others within several days. The meetings continued. Blacks, angered by our arrest, were even more determined. I went to jail 13 more times during the remaining course of the boycott, and amassed a total of $250,000 in property bonds for my release.

The white superintendent of Oakley Training School called the jail while I was locked up on one occasion. He told the sheriff to inform me that I was fired for not showing up at work. I was the school's musician, and had missed the big graduation ceremony. Big deal!

The bond of picketers grew large and included a cross-section of people. Among the most vividly remembered were: Connie Larkins Williams, a strong-willed, strong-spirited young lady. Connie had grown up in an area not far from Marcus Bottom and was angered over the lack of city services provided to her mother. (Connie, but for a little, would have led an insurrection.) Then there was Isaiah

Rembrandt, who was nicknamed "No comment," as that was his ready response to any and all questions asked of him by the news media and others. The group included Michael Sims and Welton Wardell who, as young Vietnam veterans, organized the vets' auxiliary of the Vicksburg Freedom movement, standing in as vigilant guards, ready and able to protect us. Mildred (Topsey) Cosey, through her eloquent oratorical and singing abilities, provided the inspiration needed at our most trying times. Mr. and Mrs. Eddie Thomas and their two children actively participated as a family, spending long hours on picket lines, then hurrying off to nightly mass meetings. Mrs. Mary Carter, a middle-age black woman, was known for her sharp answers and ability to think swiftly, confronting and confounding those who opposed the Freedom movement. Mr. and Mrs. Tommie Williams and Mrs. Bosley from Valley Street completed the group of regulars. Mr. Williams, although blind, aided the movement tremendously and set up a community assistance program called, "We Care Community Center." "We Care" became a resource point for many people in need of food, clothing, household articles, and money.

The concerned citizens secured the services of renowned Mississippi Civil Rights attorney R. Jess Brown and local attorney James Winfield. Both forceful, convincing, smart attorneys. They fought desperately for us and remained as trusted legal counsels. They worked unlimited hours and were willing to accept our limited funds for compensation. R. Jess Brown, then in his seventies, knew Mississippi— its deliberate sins of injustice and its calculated intentions to keep blacks as second-class citizens. James Winfield was swiftly learning that justice in Mississippi was not blind. He knew that the "good old boy legal system of Mississippi was bent on executing the full limits of Southern law on "just us" (blacks).

With criminal conspiracy changes pending for over 30 people, attorneys Brown and Winfield secured the assistance of several other black attorneys, including Jackson attorney Firnst Alexander, son of Margaret Walker Alexander, the renowned author of *Jubilee*. They also

116

sought legal assistance from the Mississippi Coalition of Lawyers, a group composed largely of white attorneys from the North.

Having lost my job at Oakley, I joined Connie Larkins and enrolled at Jackson State University to study towards the Master's degree while still actively involved in the leadership of Vicksburg's Freedom movement. The boycott waxed on for nearly two more months. White merchants of the city were hit hard. City administrators began to negotiate towards a swift resolution of our grievances.

At long last, the boycott ended. Unfortunately, our problems did not. We were summoned to court in Biloxi before Judge Nixon, who presided for the U.S. Court of Appeals. Winfield and Brown had finally advanced our appeals for relief from the impending charges that carried a maximum sentence of five years imprisonment if we were convicted.

I was one of the first witnesses called by attorney Winfield, and I answered questions relative to my involvement in the Vicksburg Freedom Movement. Judge Nixon then cross-examined me and his first question was, "Do the Chiplin's own a grocery store?" When I answered, "Yes," his second question was asked in a very hostile tone of voice. "Didn't you just purchase a second grocery store and then start the boycott for your personal gain?" I answered, "Absolutely not. Boycott business causes many problems for small store owners!" Then, in my usual sudden rush of anger, I asked Judge Nixon, "Have you not boycotted black businesses all of your life?" He sat forward, his face flush red and banged his gavel on the bench, ordering, "Step down, you flippant Negro!"

17

The Second Siege in Vicksburg

As legal appeals advanced to higher courts in our behalf, I completed the Master's program at Jackson State. We were certain that angry white merchants of Vicksburg who were finally back to business as usual, along with other diehards in the state, would find some way of getting back at us. Daddy described a period of several months after the boycott as "the calm before the storm." He knew the possibilities. We had experienced two bombings and one attempt on Momma's life. Something would happen, but what?

Life moved on under the uneasy calm. I applied for numerous jobs in Vicksburg, but was turned down. Most of the time, would-be employers told me that I was over-qualified—had too much education. Perhaps so, for a black man who would not be pushed around. The telephone rang one morning before I left for work at the store in Marcus Bottom. A white counselor for the Mississippi Employment Service informed me that he had searched all over and finally located me a job—night watchman at Westinghouse, Inc. down Highway 61. Insulted, I informed him that I didn't even watch my own house, and for sure, I was not going to watch Westinghouse. I wanted to utilize my teaching skills.

At last, the principal of Thomastown Junior/Senior High School called and asked if I would accept a position at his school, just across the Mississippi River Bridge at Thomastown, Louisiana. I accepted.

I returned home after school one evening in early September, and Momma informed me that we had received a certified letter from the Mississippi Tax Commission, ordering us to pay $50,000 in back retail taxes for the Marcus

Mr. and Mrs. Chiplin at work at Chip's Grocery, 1970.

Bottom grocery store. We had been in and out of tax controversies with the commission, but this mandate was ridiculous—contrived as a weapon to siege our business operations. For us to have owed that much in sales tax at the rate of five cents on the dollar, our retail sales for the period in question would have amounted to $1 million.

We requested an appeal, but were not granted one. Instead, the commission informed us they would be at the store on a Monday, near the beginning of October and would, if the taxes were not paid in full, padlock the doors, seizing the property for public auction. I remained home with Momma and Daddy that morning, and we waited at Chip's Grocery in Marcus Bottom.

The Tax Commission arrived around 10:00. Three white men entered the store and asked Daddy if he had the $50,000 to pay. His answer was "No." They asked us to go outside as they put a padlock on the front door and posted a "No Trespassing" sign. The leader then informed us they were headed to our second store on Openwood Street. Without further conversation, they pulled off en route to the store. Momma and Daddy rode with me. My heart pounded with anger as I deliberated what could be done to stop the Tax Commission's next seizure. Nearing the store, the answer came as a revelation from Heaven.

Corrie Lee, my brother T. J.'s wife, had opened the store and there were several customers shopping. The three white men walked into the store with me right behind them. I waited until they finished going over a court order to sieze the property of James T. and Rose Lee Chiplin and shared my revelation, "Your order is to sieze the property of James T. and Rosa L. Chiplin. Sir, this store is owned by Charles K. and James T. Chiplin—Chip and Chip's Grocery—I am Charles, and I don't owe you nothing!" My proclamation stunned them. They huddled and whispered for nearly five minutes. Advancing from the huddle, the pack leader said, "He is right. We will be in big trouble if we close this store." They turned, walked out, and slammed the door behind them as we celebrated. Like Fannie Lou Hamer, we were sick and tired of being sick and tired, but now was our moment of triumph. By the way, Daddy had transferred a substantial portion of stock from Marcus Bottom to Openwood street. He never said it, but I am sure he must have had the same notion I had..."There is more than one way to skin a cat."

Although we prevailed in keeping the Openwood Street Store, we were forever saddened by the loss of daily association with our Bottom friends. Oh well, at least we would see them at Mt. Carmel Church and stop often to sit out on their front porches. Daddy reminded us constantly to "Make new friends, but keep the old—one is silver, the other gold...friendships that have stood the test of time and chance are truly best."

120

THE BEGINNING OF SORROW

We continued to operate Chip and Chip's Grocery and continued a series of bouts with the Mississippi Tax Commission. Business was good and we later opened a restaurant next door to the store. Momma got a chance to do more of what she really liked—cooking special orders for people all across town. As business expanded, so did the need for additional employees. In addition to Chiplin grandchildren—Rosa, June Marie, and Kenneth Ray, and daughters-in-law—Corrie Lee and Viola on a part-time basis, others including Cynthia Peters, Linda Barnes, David Crosby and Earnestine Ellis were employed. Momma often paid a number of neighborhood children to do odd jobs around the store and restaurant.

As I returned home from a trip to Mississippi Valley State University with a neighbor, Joe Williams, my heart skipped beats as I saw cars filling the parking lot and extending on both sides down the street from the store. I was certain something had happened. Perhaps an accident or death. As I ran from the car, I heard the laughter of people. It was a party, a dinner party for Mr. Troy. Who but Rosa Lee Chiplin would have a party for a man considered by many to be among the least in town? Mr. Troy had no known relatives in Vicksburg, was always greasy and dirty, but Momma loved him with unconditional, unbiased love. It was his birthday, and Momma wanted it celebrated in style with her friends—men and women of low estate as well as her "well-to-do" friends. It still amazes me how she was able to assemble that many people on such a short notice. Came to mind one of the poems given us by Ms. T. J. Watson—"If you can talk with crowds, and yet not lose your virtue, if you can walk with kings, nor lose the common touch...if neither loving friend nor foe can hurt you; if all men count with you, but none too much..." (From "If" by Rudyard Kipling). Even more came to my remembrance, one of the roads from the Bottom—respect yourself and others.

Momma had grown progressively disturbed over the loss of communication with my brother, Jesse Clyde (Ray). Ray

121

had received an honorable discharge from the Army, met a companion, Idella, and taken up residence in Chicago. It was unlike Ray not to communicate with his family. We were accustomed to his periodic visits, always driving a new car and dressing extremely well. He came home to go fishing. He came home on many holidays and shared his broad smile and gutty laugh with us. But for nearly a year, we had not been able to hear from him or trace him. All kinds of thoughts, negative thoughts, pervaded as we agonized his absence. Letters to his address continued to return marked "return to sender," indicating that apparently he had moved and had left no forwarding address.

At what she frequently described as her "wit's end," Momma decided to send her sons to look for Ray in Chicago. Alfred, Sr., (Buddy), Thomas James (T. J.), James, Jr., (Boo) and I accepted the responsibility of finding our brother. We were sure by now that something was wrong and ours would not be an easy task. We left Vicksburg with our parents' blessings, prayers, and Momma's final instruction: "Bring my son home if you can." The expression on her face as we drove off was indicative of a mother's love and reflective of a mother's premonitions about her children.

The drive to Chicago was not uneventful and downright funny, particularly as Boo took his turn driving and headed us back to the South, having taken several wrong turns. Buddy was first to wake up as Boo accelerated swiftly and asked, "Boo, why are we passing through St. Louis again?" "Don't bother me, I'm driving!" Boo countered. "Yes, but in the wrong direction, Gump!" (Gump was one of Daddy's favorite labels for those who had made a serious error or whose actions were blatantly wrong.) Finally Boo stopped— right in somebody's garage. Buddy took over and we, after many lost miles, made it to Chicago.

Typically, the city was overcast with thick clouds of smog. I didn't like Chicago. I didn't like the uneasy feeling caused by the presence of black men standing atop buildings with guns in their hands. T. J. pointed out that they were members of the Black Stone Rangers. Didn't matter, I was intimidated with guns pointed in our direction. "Do you know J. C. Chiplin?" "Have you seen this man?" (showing Ray's picture). "Don't know him." "Are you the law?"— were our general questions and uncaring responses. After several hours, beating the pavement, we ran across a Chinese who spoke little English, but remembered Ray from the picture. "Oh, J. C., Chip, I see down back street," the gentleman told us. "Back street, where?" we asked. He pointed and said, "Dangerous, J. C. sleep in car—back street." Following his lead, we found our brother asleep on the back seat of a car, cold and drunk. Many memories flashed through my mind as we pulled him from the car. Although quite drunk, he knew who we were, and assured us he was not going back to Mississippi with us. No choice, we would have to keep him stone drunk and kidnap him.

As we drove back to Mississippi, I recalled Momma's words, "Bring my son home." Looking at Ray, being carried away from his former home, and knowing that life for him had taken some seriously sharp wrong turns, I was comforted by song lyrics, "It's a long, long road, with many a winding turn, we're on our way, who knows where, who knows why?... But I know he will not hinder me; he ain't heavy, he's my brother, so on we go."

Momma and Daddy warmly embraced their son as did a father from Biblical history when his son returned who had lived loosely, and spent his inheritance. Ray claimed to remain angry with us for kidnapping him and bringing him home, but we knew in our hearts, he was glad to be there— there where people loved him without regard to his situation, loved him because he was a son, brother, father, and friend. His bouts with alcohol were indicative of the fact that our family had a negative disposition to alcohol.

Daddy shared his early experience with alcohol with us one evening around the family table. "I slipped into the whiskey still when I was 14. I sat there and drank and drank until my eyes crossed," he said. We sat at attention, not having heard this story before. Continuing, he said, "I was sicker than a mule for nearly a week. Momma like to have beaten me to death. I knew then that I could not drink and was never going to fool with that stuff again."

Ray made several efforts to lay off the bottle, but he never totally gave it up. His drinking decreased, however, and he was able to go on with a productive life—working in the store part-time (he had extraordinary butcher skills) and working full-time at Grand Gulf Power Plant just outside Port Gibson, Mississippi. The old bonds of brotherhood rekindled between Ray, T. J., Boo and me. We were now reunited in Vicksburg. Jessie Lee and Johnnie had moved to Jackson, Mississippi.

Chip and Chip's Grocery flourished as far as black businesses in the South could, taking into consideration at least two factors against them: failure of banks to extend financial assistance to any substantial degree, preconceived ideas and mental conditioning from slavery that suggested that "the black man's prices were always higher, and his sugar not quite as sweet as the white man's." Even with this, our business survived largely because of Momma and Daddy's genuine dedication to the needs of the community. Momma never stopped helping and cooking for the neighbors. Daddy never stopped exerting efforts to bring about change, challenging the churches to be about God's holy call, and actively leading the Deacons Alliance into a force to be reckoned with, particularly by some selfish ministers who did not have their members' collective welfare at heart. He continued to speak of the roads from the bottom.

One Saturday afternoon as I worked in the restaurant next door to the store, Ray came in joking and jovial as usual. He stopped at the counter and said, "Old boy, if anything ever happens to me, I want you to preach my funeral." (I had accepted the call to the ministry not long before.) We laughed and I replied, "I sure will. The subject will be— Bidding My Brother Farewell." He repeated my subject and said, "That's it, that's what I want you to speak about." I didn't really consider what he had said, and walked over to the jukebox. Before I could put my quarter in, Ray pulled one from his pocked and said, punch A-6. I did and the music started: "Ever since I found Christ, there has been something in my life—makes me feel like flying away to be at rest; since my soul is Heaven bound, joys of Heaven all around, makes me feel like flying away to be at rest." I was surprised to know that Ray was aware of some gospel selections I had placed on the jukebox. Oh well, that was Ray—always full of surprises, keeping you on your toes. We sat a table and he said, "Thanks for kidnapping me back home. For awhile there I had strayed from the path Momma and Daddy put me on—but it's all right now."

Later that night, I went over into the house and heard Ray talking, pleading to Momma. I walked close to the dining room door and saw him down on his knees beside her chair saying, "Whatever I have done wrong in the past, please forgive me...I love you, gal." Momma pulled him close and embraced him as in former days, reassuring that she loved him too.

Two weeks later, in June of 1976 around 11:00, Momma came into the restaurant, embraced me, and said, "It's all over, he's dead!" The first thing I thought was Daddy was dead before she started crying out Ray's name. Uncle Red had just called to inform us that the Sheriff of Port Gibson asked him to come out and identify Ray who had been run over by a car as he walked on Highway 61 south. He had taken off from work and was headed to Fayette to see Aunt Shug (Momma's sister) and Uncle Red. No doubt he expected to get a ride somewhere along the highway for the 20 mile distance.

The words "Old boy, if anything happens to me, preach my funeral" resounded in my mind as I listened to the sheriff's account of the hit-and-run accident. "It appears that Mr. Chiplin (Ray) was walking alongside Highway 61 South down from Port Gibson and was struck by a car driven by Mrs. Washington, wife of Dr. Walter Washington, President of Alcorn College. Mrs. Washington called my office a couple of hours later and reported that she hit something on the highway but was afraid to stop. By then, Mr. Chiplin's body had been identified and the funeral home from Fayette had picked him up."

"The beginnings of sorrow"—for the first time in the history of our immediate family, we had a need to purchase a cemetery plot; for the first time we would stand at graveside and bid farewell to a close loved one.

Daddy entrusted the arrangements to Jefferson Funeral Home. They did not inform him that they drew samples of Ray's blood to send for testing in an attempt by Mrs. Washington's defense lawyer to clear her of the criminal, hit-and-run charges. As far as we were concerned, nothing could restore the loss of a brother, a friend who was trying so hard to get his life together. It helped us to know that Ray had gravitated back to the roads that Daddy and Momma led him to early in life.

His was a beautiful service in the Chapel of Jefferson Funeral Home. Our long-time friend, William Tripplet sang a consoling song, enthralling the chapel with his rich, melodic tenor voice. "Be still my soul, the Lord is on thy side; bear patiently, the cross of grief and pain; leave to thy God to order and provide; in every change, He faithful will remain."

After the song, I stood, announced the sermon title Ray and I had agreed on: "Bidding My Brother Farewell," and eulogized him. There was a lot of comforting truth to share about Ray, about life and about God.

It took over a year for me to bring myself not to go to Ray's grave several times per week. Momma often wept at night after closing the store. No criminal charges were filed against Mrs. Washington; we, however, filed civil charges with the representation of attorney Kenneth Middleton, our first cousin Claudine's husband. An out-of-court settlement was offered and accepted, as we only desired to go on with our lives, ever praying for God's strength to fully forgive Mrs. Washington and hoping that she would find forgiveness for herself.

I went to study towards the doctorate in education at Northeast Louisiana University in Monroe, Louisiana the next school year after Ray's death. I drove to and from Monroe daily for three years as I was still needed at the store and restaurant. Business remained good, but our battles with the State Tax Commission continued. Momma and Daddy knew full well that they would never be fair with us again. They weren't, and often sent threatening certified letters for tax collections that had already been paid in full, although outrageously high.

In the summer of 1979, I was employed as Director of Activities for the Division of Student Services at Jackson State University. Although only nine hours short of completing the doctorate, I needed to take an additional job to help pay the ongoing unfair taxes. I signed my check each month and gave it to my parents to help out without any hesitation or regret. I believed in the business and was willing to do whatever it took to keep it going.

Ray's death signaled a period of grief that spanned at least four years. In 1978, Daddy's mother (Anney) died at a nursing home. We had tried to keep her at home with us, particularly after her several attempts to burn wood on her gas stove. When we moved her in, many of her antiques and family relics had been swindled by white collectors who took advantage of her mental fragility. Her episodes of wandering away from our house onto dangerous thoroughfares dictated the need for professional care and attention.

Anney's death marked the loss of Daddy's one, closest biological relative, excluding his children. He was a strong man, however, and found solace in his recollections of her teachings and the funny things she used to do. For instance, he reminded us that once, after leaving Anney behind in Jefferson County, one of her close friends died. Anney wrote him, requesting that he come and help with the funeral as he historically had done for many people, utilizing his written and verbal skills. Her letter read: "Dear son, please come home and read (as she tried to spell) "the 'obitchaway'." Now, top that one.

The recent loss of a son and mother never seemed to break Daddy's spirit. He was determined that his community would change and continued his strong orations in that regard. He became an "outcast" to many black preachers in Vicksburg who felt threatened by his verbal attacks on their leadership as pastors, reminding them that "no man can write his name so high in the sands that time will not erase it." His belief in the collective economy of the black community grew stronger, and he made an attempt to assemble other black store owners, suggesting that we could come together, pool resources and purchases wholesale in bulk quantities and thereby pass savings along to the customers. At least one meeting of black store owners was held at our house where Daddy suggested, "If we set up a warehouse, we could buy boxcar loads of a number of products—these purchases would be at much lower cost than we now pay even wholesale as individual small store owners." The several blacks who attended knew that he was right, but never brought themselves to move on his proposal. Unfortunately, their business perspective was dimmed by southern mentalities that created barriers to the progress and survival of black business—limited trust for each other; the unexplained need to stand alone; and most acutely—complacency and sentiment with "business as usual." His seventy years of life experiences in the Black community made him readily aware of the previous and he knew his proposal had fallen on deaf ears. None the less, he continued to work hard at his business, expanding to add a game room which, with so many children in the neighborhood, was very successful. He and Momma spent many hours figuring out ways to offer specials to their customers, many of whom still carried grocery accounts. They circulated sales flyers into the community for the store and restaurant. Everyone knew, however, that their most abundant commodity was love, and that it was offered without charge.

18

A Lesson in History

Sixteen years following the founding of the Deacon's Alliance of Vicksburg. Daddy made an annual address commemorating the organization's continued role in the struggle for freedom. He proudly stood and said:

Honorable Pastor of this beloved Grove Street Baptist Church, officers, members and friends, it is with profound gratitude that I, as president of this Deacon's Alliance, greet you on this our 16th birthday. There has not been a Saturday since we began that we didn't have our class. We want our record to be established in the hearts of men, so when children yet unborn ask the question, "What was the Deacon's Alliance?" the story can be told them of what took place in the South in the 1960s... We can ride through the National Park here in this city and see tablets of stone and monuments of stone telling us what happened here in the 1860s during the War Between the States...One general said "war is hell." We who came through the struggle in the '60s can attest to that statement. We endured a great deal of suffering, even death. Many lives were lost for what we are enjoying today....Now, Satan has unleashed his tyrannic power here in Mississippi and the South....The churches are no hiding place.... When the freedom fight grew strong here in the '60s, there were no deacon statesmen in the city and no preachers like Paul. The mad waters of human passion were dashing against our Christian fortress and it seemed like nothing could calm the tide...I called a meeting of my fellow deacons at Mt. Carmel Church at a time when McBride and Charles were being criticized by the local pastors for their leadership in the crisis. I wanted to remind the deacons and pastors that there was still power in the blood and that the freedom movement was a cornerstone to be established in the heart of Christians....I reminded us through the words of the song which says—"Must I be carried to the skies on flowery beds of ease, while others fought to win the prize and sail through bloody seas? Are there no foes for me to face; must I not stem the flood? Is this vile world a friend to grace to help me on to God? Surely I must fight if I shall reign, increase my courage Lord; I'll bear the toil, endure the pain, supported by Thy Word."

The moving eloquence of Daddy's speech inspired the capacity crowd and more importantly, reminded me of who he was—no slave or indentured servant to Jake Wagoner or any other plantation owner, but a smart, caring black man who could even make a stubborn old mule plow.

James Taft Chiplin, Sr., 1987.

In addition to running the store, Momma's preoccupation was her grandchildren. Most of them were into their teens. Kenneth Ray completed Temple High and decided to enlist in the Army. Having been promised computer technology as his military assignment, and instead having been sent straight to the front line in Vietnam, he wrote and asked our assistance in getting him a hardship release from the Army. I went directly to Senator Stennis' office and arrangements were made immediately to send him home. After that he worked as a fireman in Vicksburg, and continued to help at the store. Momma's devotion for her daughters-in-law, past (from four of my brothers' divorces) and present reminded us of the bond between Ruth and her daughter-in-law Naomi, who in Biblical recording told Ruth, "Entreat me not to leave thee, nor to return from following after thee; for whither thou goest, I will go, and wither thou lodgest, I will lodge; thy people shall be my people, and Thy God, my God." Somehow, with this embedded in their hearts, Bertha (Boo's ex-wife), Viola (Buddy's ex-wife), Corrie Lee (T. J.'s ex-wife) and Alice (Edward Lee's ex-wife) remained close to Momma and the family, relishing their positions not as ex-daughters-in-law, but daughters. The Chiplin grandchildren learned a lot from their grandparents. They had seen them right there in times of need. They knew and respected their instructions to their children (their parents) and additionally sought their advice and used it.

Divorces in the family had never broken deep family ties. Momma and Daddy still regarded Ruth Dunlap as a sister although she and Momma's brother, Edward, were divorced and had earlier invited her to stay with us during her beginning years of teaching in Vicksburg. Ruth returned the love and was a favorite of neighborhood children particularly because she played basketball with them out back when school was out, sealing the bond that was so desperately needed and appreciated.

Momma's sister's health began to decline as she experienced the onset of Alzheimer's disease. We were heartbroken to see the intelligent, talented, caring teacher, Aunt Shug, rapidly lose memory. She had invested and given so much, not only towards the education of black children in Fayette, but for the well-being of everybody, most certainly our family. While grieved, Momma respected God's will for her life and endeavored to assist as much as she could.

Blacks in Vicksburg, although hired in some managerial positions, given better positions on the police department and, receiving somewhat better city services, had not "overcome" nor "arrived." Momma suggested that we should begin a breakfast club. She called the first meeting at our house and was overwhelmed with that early Sunday morning response. Mrs. Thelma Rush, Mr. and Mrs. Tripplet, Mrs. Ledora Marley, Mrs. Rosie Middleton Durman, Ms. Linda Barnes, Mrs. Geneva Powell, attorney James Winfield, Robert Walker, Melvin Redmond (who had been elected as a city alderman through Momma's efforts), Ruth Dunlap and others attended. Among the many concerns of that group was the fostering of improved education and providing incentives for black children to strive harder in school. With the participation of an overflow crowd, the American Legion Hut became the next and permanent meeting site for the Vicksburg Breakfast Club. Meetings were held at 7:00 each second Sunday morning. As usual, Momma cooked and hauled breakfast fit for kings and queens to the meetings. With mass meetings now in the distant past, the club became another community sounding board, watching and monitoring strides towards more freedom and equality.

In addition to the Breakfast Club, Momma earlier joined the Ladies Modernistic Club which proved to be an excellent social outlet for her. Her good friends for many years— Rosa Washington, Nannie Franklin, Laura Bolton, Eloise Smith, Gertrude Carrington, Earnestine Ellis and others— were members of the organization that held its monthly meetings at various members' homes. They had fun sharing jokes and tall tales and competed in their culinary skills. Additionally, she joined the Vicksburg Professional Women's Club, shared and benefited from their business forums and community projects. She was well accepted by and readily adjusted to people from all walks of life. I really don't believe she ever considered anyone she met as a stranger. To her, it was another person worth knowing and worth taking up time with.

Daddy's affiliations were many. He took every opportunity to join meaningful organizations, believing that "in unity there is strength." A natural leader, he held offices in the D. W. Simmon's Brotherhood Relief Club, Sunday School Convention, Deacon's Alliance, was for many years Worshipful Master of Stringer Lodge #1 at Vicksburg and Grand Senior Warden for the Most Worshipful Stringer Grand Lodge, Free and Accepted Masons in the State of Mississippi. He often told us that a black man should first join the church, then the Masons. We saw Masonry at work in his life as he was a man "standing on the square, plumbing the line." We saw him sit up all night with sick masonic brothers and often attend the urgent needs of their children and widows. For instance...A knock at the front door after midnight. A Masonic brother from the North, seeking assistance, stands there. "You Mr. Chiplin?" When Daddy answered, "Yes," the proper Masonic greeting was shared and soon the night visitor, his wife and three small children sat at the table eating. Naturally, Momma insisted. Their car had stopped and they needed financial assistance. They got it. Daddy would have helped regardless of his Masonic affiliation.

Boo, Wansley (Jessie's husband) and I were inducted into Stringer Lodge on the same night in 1972. It didn't take long for us to realize the strength and importance of the organization and to understand why Daddy did many of the things he did. In 1979, Daddy received his 40 year service pin from the Grand Lodge. The late H. M. Thompson proudly presented it to him and spoke of his unusual knowledge of Masonry and Masonic history. H. M. depended on Daddy and regularly invited him to take trips all over the world in their Masonic work.

19

Setting of the Sun

On Saturday, March 15, 1980, Momma and Daddy decided to take a day off from business and spend some time with Jessie, her husband Wansley, and their three boys— Brian, Ary and Kevin—in Jackson, Mississippi. I stopped by Jessie's house after work at Jackson State University around 1:30 p.m. Daddy sat watching T.V. with Wansley and the children, Momma rested on the sofa and Jessie brought up the late noon meal. They were so happy to have their parents with them for a day and they were equally glad to be there. Momma went into her purse, pulled out $10, put it in my hand and said, "Put this in your pocket... Your always giving everybody else and walking around with nothing in your pocket." She was right—I got that from her. Following the meal, I said bye and headed to Vicksburg to work in the restaurant.

It started out to be a normal business evening until around 6:30. June Marie, my niece, entered the restaurant and said, "Uncle Charles, Grandma just had a heart attack!" Tons of bricks seemingly dropped in my heart. As I rushed next door to the house, I saw them driving hurriedly away to the hospital. Momma's heart malfunction had erupted an aneurism of a major artery leading to the heart.

I had seen her sick before, but never this sick. Teams of doctors swarmed in and out of her room at Mercy Regional Medical Center, working frantically. We waited, numb and heartbroken, for her slightest sign of improvement. She did not improve. Johnnie Mae insisted that she should be moved immediately to the University Medical Center at Jackson and made necessary arrangements. Lasting is the memory of how Momma looked as Kenneth Ray assisted in placing her in the ambulance. Kenneth had transferred to the emergency division of the Vicksburg Fire Department. As he drove off, Momma Lucy turned to me and asked, "You think my daughter is going to be alright?" I gave her the answer she wanted to hear, but felt deep in my heart that Momma would not return to Vicksburg alive.

For nearly two months, Johnnie and Jessie rotated around-the-clock stays with Momma. Johnnie pulled back-to-back shifts, relieving Jessie during those times when Momma's condition was worse. Johnnie's position as a head nurse at the Medical Center facilitated a number of vital services. Daddy and I continued to run the business and traveled back and forth to Jackson daily.

Around noon on May 1, 1980, as I sat in my office at JSU, tired and half napping, Momma's voice (I'm certain in my daydream) sounded distinctly, saying, "Charles, I can't live like this." I shared the experience with other family members and suggested that we begin to pray for strength to accept God's will for her.

On the night of May 9, 1980, we received a call at the store in Vicksburg, informing us that they had coded Momma and asking us to remain close by the phone. Within an hour, Shirley Williams, a longtime family friend, neighbor, and claim daughter of Momma and Daddy's came to our house and told us, "Your Momma didn't make it." What do you say? What do you do? How do you feel? Nothing makes sense. Light seems dark, up seems down, cold seems hot, when your mother dies. So, what did we do at that longest moment in the recorded memory of our souls— got the family Bible, turned to Psalms 121 and read: "I will lift up my eyes unto the hills from whence cometh my strength." It came.

Momma's funeral was a mirror of the person she was and the life she had lived. She had visited the imprisoned, clothed the naked, fed the hungry, attended the sick and afflicted. She had helped a lot of people as she passed along, cheered a lot of people with her words and songs, and told some people when they were traveling wrong, and certainly, her life had not been in vain. They were all there—the poor, the needy, the well-to-do, aristocrats, city dignitaries, city fathers, freedom workers, freedom deniers—they came to pay respect at Mt. Carmel to the lady who had looked beyond the faults of many and seen their needs. We were once more consoled by William Tripplet, who sang one of her favorite songs, "There's a garden where Jesus is waiting; there's a place that is wondrously fair—for it glows with the light of His presence, 'tis the beautiful garden of prayer." We sat proudly and listened to many tributes paid in Momma's memory. Patrick Stirgus and the Bethel A.M.E. Church choir sang a stirring rendition of "Going Up to Yonder" and the music program was completed by Dan Ethel Edwards who encouraged us with the following: "If you just hold out until tomorrow, if you just keep the faith through the night; if you just hold out until tomorrow, everything will be alright. In my life, I've had my share of sorrows, but the darkest hour comes just before day; so many nights I've had to lay down and face tomorrow, knowing that the Lord will make a way."

Scores of people lined the sidewalks as Momma was carried from Marcus Bottom and across town to City Cemetery. As the family car drove up Halls Ferry Road, my mind reflected on what she and Daddy had identified as roads from the bottom, and I was comforted to know that she had traveled each one of them: Know yourself; respect yourself and others; have faith; get a good education; never give up; associate with people who are trying to advance; help somebody else; stand up for something; trust in God and pray daily.

On the next morning after Momma's funeral, Daddy and I had breakfast together and shared heart to heart. "Rosa is resting with Jesus now, Charles. We have to go on. There is so much she would want us to continue," Daddy said as he slowly ate. Following his comments, I said to him, "Daddy, you're still alive. I don't want you to throw in the towel now. Please be happy." Although we know he was torn with grief, Daddy went on, still whistling and humming as he sought to continue the business. He was strong. Strong enough to return Momma's choir robe to the church the next day and unveil her chair. Marking the chair of a deceased member with a black bow for a 90-day mourning period is traditional for many black Baptist churches in the South. Daddy said, "Rosa would give up her seat for someone to sit down; why should they keep others from sitting there now? She has a seat in His kingdom."

TIME TO MOVE ON

Not many months after Momma died, as Daddy had celebrated his 72nd birthday with unbent determination to serve his fellow man, he decided to lease the store and move to Clinton, Mississippi, closer to his daughters at Jackson. Difficulties with the Tax Commission had continued. Since I was a partner in my father's business, the tax commission secured a garnishment on my checks from Jackson State University for a period of nearly three years. I was relieved that finally my father could enjoy his latter years in peace, away from the business. I knew that he would not be content to sit and do nothing. That most definitely was not one of his roads.

Moving to Jackson did not change any of his religious, fraternal, and social affiliations in Vicksburg. He continued to visit home at least three times each week, was there for meetings and attended church services regularly at Mt. Carmel. Something about Vicksburg engrossed his spirit and his heart. Marcus Bottom was his endeared home, although he had moved away to Openwood Street before Momma died. He held on to many dreams of change— good change for the Bottom, hoping that some day blacks who lived there would once more unite, open more productive businesses, and improve the general economy of the area. He spoke often of good work ethics that should be utilized not only by people of Marcus Bottom, but anywhere in this nation.

In reference to his concept of work, Daddy delivered a speech to the Deacon's Alliance, wherein he said:

My subject today is Drones in the Master's bee hive. A drone is said to be a lazy bee. All a drone does is serve in the reproductive department, fertilizing the queen's eggs. The workers are those who are found busy every sunny day, gathering not only from the flowers, but from places where waste is found—outdoor toilets, latrines, or whatever. They can extract something that they mix with other ingredients to produce the honey we like so well.... After gathering their load of materials, they fly to their hive where they complete the process of converting their load into that which they will defend with their lives, honey. Just how that waste material is converted into honey is a secret only the honey bees know, a secret they have kept since it was given to them by the Great Creator. The work of the worker bee is unified all over the world—the honey they produce is the same from hive to hive, has the same texture, and is never over or under proportion. Fortunately, the worker bee (honey manufacturing engineer) knows when the work is complete—knows when it stops.

I suggest that we black people should remove ourselves from existence as only lazy drones (agents only of reproduction) and advance to become workers....The Scriptures teach that man will live by the sweat of his brow.

Into his eighties, James Chiplin, Sr. continued to study.

Daddy's influence was felt through his insistent on those in positions of leadership to fulfill in their responsibility to mankind. He continued to accept speaking engagements in Vicksburg and other cities across Mississippi. He was hailed as "Mr. Chiplin, the wise, self-taught educator and lecturer." I simply saw him as a man who continued to travel roads from the bottom.

Speaking of world peace, Daddy said in one address:

> Every gun that is made, every military arsenal, every rocket fired, signifies in the final summation, a theft from those who are hungry and not fed, those who are cold and not clothed. This world at arms is not only spending money as it stock-piles weapons of war, it is spending the sweat of its society, labors of its geniuses, its scientists and the hopes of its children...This is not a way of life at all, in any true sense of decency. Under a cloud of war, humanity hangs from a cross of iron.

20

The Bottom Revisited

In June of 1991, Daddy and I attended a Masonic service in Vicksburg. After the service, he wanted to go down to the Bottom. With no pressing schedules, we took a great deal of time visiting our old stomping ground. At first glance everything looked the same, but closer observation revealed a nightmare of horrors that were depressing—symbols and signs of satanic gangs had been carefully sprayed on numerous buildings. Most available wall spaces bore messages—"KILL!" "ALL IS WELL!" "IVL" (Insane Vice Lords), etc. Windows and doors of many houses were secured with iron bars. It was Sunday evening, but unlike in former days, many young people stood out on the corners with beer cans and moved to deafening rock music from their car or truck radios. Two young men about 16, stopped cars after flashing signs revealing that they were drug pushers.

We went to Miss Gistina's house and after the usual exchange of greetings, listened to her summation of the new Marcus Bottom. "Brother Chiplin, I tell you , this is not the same bottom you raised your children up in. People have let their children run wild—don't care about what they do...Us old folks scared to go down the street even in the daytime." Her sister Francis shared, "People talk about how hard it is to make children act right because they are single parents. There were many single parents in the Bottom years back—my mother was one of them. (Miss Luela, the lady who had supported her family by taking in laundry.) We knew that when Momma said no, she meant no. We respected her and all adults—you remember how it was."

We left Miss Gistina's and stopped by Mrs. Lee Willa Millers for a quick visit. She also spoke of the overwhelming

As Mr. Chiplin saw the Bottom in 1991. Gang activity has intensified.

problems, sharing, "Many of the children don't go to school now. They hang around and get in trouble. It breaks my heart. I am ailing now, but I call them over to my fence and tell them how so many of us worked to improve things for black folks. I make them say, 'Yes ma'am' to me."

Sorrow gripped Daddy's being as we drove away. My heart was broken as he reflected:

> Your Momma and I did the best we could to bring our children up right. We talked to you about some roads that would lead from the bottom—not moving from the bottom necessarily. You see, the bottom is not where you live, but how you live...Marcus Bottom has some great people who have never left. It now has some people who are living at the bottom—drinking on the streets on Sunday, selling dope, hurting and killing people in gangs, painting terrible things on people's walls. Never thought I'd live to see the day it would be like this...After integration, some black folks thought they should keep up with the Joneses and forgot to teach their

children and to love their children. Now they are afraid of those same darling souls they brought into the world.

We drove on past young people on the streets and heard profanity spoken loudly. There were children wearing expensive designer clothes, but they appeared very sloppy. I remembered how we were not allowed to leave the house with a shirttail out. The Bottom appeared strange and dangerous. As we drove away Daddy said, "Train up a child in the way he should go while he is young, and when he is old, he will not depart." Then with perfect recall, he recited a poem by an unknown author:

> I may never be as clever as my neighbor down the street;
> I may never be as prominent as some men I meet.
>
> I may never have the things that some men have had;
> But I've got to be successful as a little fellow's dad.
>
> I may never come to glory, I may never have gold;

Former participants in "second chance," an inmate rehabilitation program organized by Charles Chiplin and Hinds County Sherrif, Malcolm McMillin. Also shown are volunteers.

Men may count me as a failure when my business
   life is told.

But the one task I'm set on—is the job I work at most;
If I failed that growing youngster, I'll have nothing
   else to boast.

Although wealth and fame I'd gather, all my future
   would be sad—
If I failed to be successful as that little fellow's dad.

A NEW KIND OF MOVEMENT

On June 6, 1992, Daddy called me at home late in the
evening. He said, "The sheriff has been looking for you!"
"For me? For what?" I questioned. Shifting his tone, he
said, "Sheriff McMillin talked with me at length about a
program he wants to get started at the jail out in Raymond.
He wants to give those men a chance to turn their lives
around. Says he thought about starting a choir and some
other activities that will help to rehabilitate them. I told
him that you are the right man for the job. It doesn't pay,
but your reward will be great in the Master's kingdom. Can
I give him your telephone number?" I responded yes. Daddy
hung up and shortly Sheriff McMillin called. After he explained what his intentions for the Hinds County Farm were,
I told him I would be happy to work with his program.

Within several days, the sheriff arranged for our first meeting with inmates at the chapel of the farm. About 12 showed
up. McMillin decided to use his authority as sheriff and
scheduled another meeting the next day, ordering all inmates
of the jail to attend. Certainly they did; after all, he was the
sheriff.

We knew very well that most people had some previous
religious experiences in their background and could share
through a common language—gospel music. We were right.
The songs touched them in unexplainable ways. Men serving short sentences for minor crimes and men serving sentences in excess of 10 years for major crimes raised their
voices in song together. The sheriff agreed with the sugges-
tion of one inmate, Keith Brown, to name the choir and its
related activities "**Second Chance**."

Daddy called several times each week for an update on how Second Chance was doing. He was so proud to know that he had once again assisted a human need. "Charles, God gives us all another chance every day. None of us could stand His justice. It is only through His mercy that we endure," he pointed out. I was absolutely aware of God's unlimited mercy and His granting of second, third, fourth and beyond fifth chances. There were times that I too had drifted from the good roads from the bottom and had encounters with alcohol. At the time I started working with the sheriff's program, I had made a deep inward decision not to not drink. I have not to this date.

Remembering what Daddy had told us of his boyhood experience with alcohol and knowing how my brothers and I were adversely effected through its usage, I understood the plight and desperation of many of the inmates. Many were victims of drug addictions. There are no winners with drugs. I was also reminded of the movie, "Cotton Comes to Harlem" with Redd Foxx and others as efforts were contrived to put drugs in black communities to destroy them. More saddening was the realization that to a large effect, the sabotage had been unsuccessful. I also remembered that in earlier times in Marcus Bottom, beyond the drug alcohol, the use of the term drug referred to across-the-counter medications, particularly B.C., Stanback and Goody's headache powders.

In addition to serious addictions facilitated by the availability of dangerous drugs in our communities, I was aware that many of the inmates were victims of America's failed economic system. Many who had sought employment had been continuously told to "Check back in a few days," "We'll get back in touch" and the like. Many black men, although collectively labeled irresponsible, wanted badly to be bread-winners for their families, wanted to be respected as fathers and did not want their families on welfare.

One thing was very clear to me—Daddy had gotten me involved with one of the greatest challenges of my life, and I was determined to master it. I had been schooled in the Scriptures and what real Christianity was about. I was mindful of the fact that "All have sinned and come short of the glory of God."

After the first few meetings of Second Chance, the sheriff informed me that I would be in charge from then on and he would visit and assist as often as possible. The numbers grew larger as more men were locked up, particularly black men.

I made every effort to remind the scores of inmates—blacks, whites and others—that a man's freedom is priceless and that we should do all in our power to remain free. Inasmuch as they were physically bound, they were encouraged to remain free in their minds and spirits, not reverting to the mental chains that helped perpetuate slavery in America for hundreds of years.

A member of our church asked me, "Aren't you afraid to go out to the jail and work with the criminals?" My ready reply was, "No. I am more afraid to work with some people in the churches who profess to be Christians, but hang around in their 'church gangs' talking about people and destroying them with their sharp tongues." Came to mind the passage of scripture: "I was hungry and you fed me not; naked, and you clothed me not; imprisoned, and you visited me not."

21

The Best of Times/The Worst of Times

Much of Daddy's leisure time was filled with writing speeches and poems. He wrote "My Tracks" as a tribute and challenge to his children and "Trouble At Sea" for motivation during these troubled times. He felt that his children and grandchildren would do well to bring their children up as he had brought us up—with respect, love and the fear of God.

MY TRACKS
Dedicated to my children
James T. Chiplin, Sr.

As I travel day by day
I put down tracks and leave them to stay.
All the way there and all the way back
Everywhere I go, I leave my tracks.

Out in the world or in my home
Whether with company or all alone.
I leave my tracks, but what does it mean
If straight tracks cannot be seen.

So since I must make tracks at any rate
I will try my best to make them straight.
As for me, I can't afford
To leave my tracks on a downward road.

If I go to the gambling den
My tracks are left to be seen by men.
If I go to the ballroom floor,
My tracks are left right there in the door.

146

But when I kneel at home in family prayer
You can also find my footprints there.
When I go to church to worship God,
My footprints are planted in the churchyard.

To make straight tracks, I must sacrifice
And follow along in the footprints of Christ.
Because further up the road, I'm bound to look back
And see my child stepping in my tracks.

Then I don't want to regret
The tracks that I made
I want to be happy
With the pattern I've laid.

TROUBLE AT SEA
James T. Chiplin, Sr.

Master, the tempest is raging
The waters are dashing across the bough.
We tried hard to reach the land
But Master, we don't see how.
We tried not to disturb you dear Master
We know nothing else to do.
We want you to see Dear Savior
What we are going through.

The Master looked at the conditions
He had the power in His hand
To speak to the wind and the water
And bring them under His command.
He said to the wind "Peace"
To the water He said "Be Still."
But the men, I'm training them
To do my father's will.
The howling winds stopped blowing
The angry sea became calm.

The disciples' fears were relieved
But they were resting in Jesus' arms.

When the storms of life are raging
Be sure Jesus is on your ship
He'll calm your troubled water
When the waves begin to rip.

Causes and cures remained Daddy's focus in 1992. By age 83 he had joined several other civic organizations inclusive of the Odd Fellows Club in Clinton and was a member of the Volunteer Club of the Hinds County Sheriff's Department. He also had organized a weekly Bible class and Senior Citizens Singing Group in Clinton. (He never considered himself a senior citizen. Age for him meant numbers and more wisdom).

He enjoyed the nicer things of life because he had managed to "put up a dry stick for a wet day." Additionally, his children did not want him in need of anything. Johnnie lav-

James Chiplin, flanked by family members, at his 82nd birthday dinner.

148

ished him with gifts, including a car. Jessie made many purchases to make his house comfortable. His sons and grandchildren made regular contributions. Each payday, I slipped money under his door. Ours were deliberate attempts "not to forget the bridge that brought us over."

On Daddy's birthday, November 16, 1992, we gave him a surprise birthday breakfast at his house. Everybody showed up there early that Sunday morning bearing gifts. He had commented earlier about a recliner Johnnie had purchased for her house. He got one. His color T.V. was several years old. He got a new larger one. The gift list was long as usual and his usual money tree was laden with cash. No words can describe the sparkle in his eyes and the joy of his heart as he held great-grandchildren, tussled with grandchildren and watched his children return the love he and Momma had given us.

Our Grand Lodge convened in Jackson during the fourth weekend in November, 1992. Daddy had not missed a Grand Session in 50 years and would not miss this one. I went down to pick him up each morning and he stood there waiting and ready to go. Although episodes of pain in his leg caused him to use a cane, he strutted proudly, twirling the cane as he whistled.

He was greeted with respect and was held in high esteem by Masonic brothers and sisters, young and old. He knew the Masonic rituals, but above that, lived each noble principle, standing on the square with all men and women. As we walked into Grand Master Bridge's office, they immediately exchanged jokes about old age and their lives as bachelors. Just as his predecessor, H. M. Thompson, Grand Master Bridges held Daddy close to his heart, trusted and respected him, benefited from his wisdom, and admired his strength and courage. Daddy's feelings for him were the same.

Grand Lodge adjourned shortly after noon on the following Tuesday. Having shared parting words, and leaving with Grand Master Bridges' motivational chant, "Fired Up and Ready to Go!" Daddy and I left for his home in Clinton. We had talked many times before, but there was something spe-

149

cial about this time. Daddy literally called the roll of his children and grandchildren and pointed out something positive about each of them..."Jessie Lee got her Master's and is a licensed mental health clinician; T. J. is doing fine in the cab business, I asked him to succeed me as worshipful Master of the Lodge back home; Buddy has done well, retired now in Alabama, living good; Johnnie Mae, that gal is something else, went on to head two floors at the University Medical Center; Boo making it good; Edward Lee and his wife are X-ray technicians...the chips off the old block, all my grands moving ahead—Marcus is a dentist; Linda, a doctor; Denise, an R.N.; Rosa working as a nurse; Bobby, Ricky, Sandy and Charles Anthony have good jobs; Anthony Troy has a good plumbing business; Ary, Brian and Kevin Taft in college, they got an eye for business, they'll do very well; Rose Mary in R.N. school; Junior (Buddy's son) has his Ph.D. in theology and law degree; Jewel working on her doctorate; Lucille has her Master's in city planning and is doing well

Having traveled granddaddy's "roads," Dr. Lynda F. Jackson Assaud receives her M.D. at Howard Medical School.

in Texas; Derrick is fine, Billy has his own business; Sharon is a master chef; Kenny Ray is working for the government; Junior (Edward Lee's son) and Terry doing fine in Houston; Annette has finished her schooling at Southern; Lisa and Leslie in school there now; and that Gerald, bless his heart, that's my boy, Gerald just won't listen." (Johnnie's son, Gerald, was then serving time in prison for accessory to a felony). Daddy paused for a moment as I waited for him to continue..."You can take a horse to water, but you can't make him drink...the horse has to be thirsty. I hope that that boy will get thirsty for what is right." I realized that Daddy had left me out of his roll call, but dared not mention it. Then, shortly up the road, before we reached Clinton, he said, "You have a big responsibility ahead of you...I want you to put a headstone on my Momma's grave at Vicksburg and while you're at it, put one on my grave too." I looked over at him and said, "Why would you want to crawl under a tombstone and you're still alive?" "Oh, I don't know. When I die, you, my baby boy, should preach my funeral," he said as I gripped the steering wheel tightly. "That's enough of that talk, Daddy," I said quietly. "You have no idea of how strong you are Charles, you will be even stronger," was his final comment before we reached our destination.

The following Sunday, Johnnie invited us to dinner at her house after church. We were excited about the recent Christmas Cantata at Cade Chapel Church where she was the narrator. After dinner, Daddy walked over to the piano and played "What a Friend We Have In Jesus," then returned to his seat at the table. As Johnnie cleared the table he said, "I want to be with Rosa one of these Christmases, all of you on the right road now—moving ahead, I sure would like a Christmas in Glory." Neither Johnnie nor I responded. I knew he would as always, have his way.

On Tuesday, December 22, 1992, Daddy delivered an address for a Senior Citizens group in Jackson. He shared the joys of the season in his usual, stirring eloquence. After saying his final words—"My heart is happy." Daddy fell to the floor. He was gone to spend his first Christmas in heaven.

Seemingly it rained from the moment Daddy died until the time of his funeral at Bethel A.M.E. Church, the birthplace of Masonry for the state of Mississippi. The church overran with people from across the state—Masonic delegations, members of mine and Johnnie's church at Jackson, Cade Chapel, friends from the Bottom and the multitude of Chiplin children, grandchildren and great grandchildren.

The sunlight struck in magnificence through the massive stained glass windows of Bethel as Johnnie stood and eloquently gave an eulogistical tribute to Daddy.

Following Johnnie's moving tribute, Mandy Strong, an administrator in the Clinton Public School System, and close friend of the family sang one of Daddy's favorite songs. The sweetness of her voice consoled us as she sang with spirit:

> As I journey through the land, singing as I go; pointing souls to Calvary and the crimson flow; Many arrows pierce my heart from without, within; but my Lord, leads me on; Through Him I must win...O' I want to see Him, look upon His face; there to sing forever of His saving grace. On the streets of Glory, let me lift my voice, cares all past, home at last; ever to rejoice.

After playing the organ, my next task was to fulfill Daddy's request—preach my funeral sermon. To follow are excerpts from the eulogy I delivered for my father.

> It's easy enough to be happy when life goes by like a song-
> But the man worthwhile is the man who will smile
> When everything goes wrong.

> It's easy enough to be prudent when nothing tempts to stray-
> When without nor within, no voice of sin is luring your soul away.

> For the test of the heart is trouble, and it always comes with the years-
> But the smile that is worth the treasures of this earth-
> is the smile that shines through the tears.

> "And I said: O' that I had wings like a dove,
> For then would I fly away, and be at rest.

152

Lo, then would I wander far off,
And remain in the wilderness.

I would hasten my escape from the windy storm and
tempest."
(Psalm 55:6-8)

GONE HOME ON THE WINGS OF A DOVE

On November 16, 1908, a boy child was born to Edith
Sanxton in Jefferson County. In due time he advanced from
crawling and tried his first steps on his feet. This monu-
mental task accomplished, he soon learned that wood plank
floors can be awfully cold on winter mornings as chilling
southern winds made wooden shutters slam back and forth
against a plantation house sheltered from the rain by a tin
roof.

He learned to accept the taste and smell of drinking water in old tin barrels that had collected from the rain.

He soon learned that children born without silver spoons
in their mouths and who were also recent descendants of
black men and women who had not long relished freedom,
experienced lives in nothing close to a bed of roses—did not
bask in the sun while their parents sipped lemonade, lightly
gliding back and forth in swings on porches that almost en-
compassed their houses.

Rather, he learned to respond obediently to the commands
of Edith's voice as she called out to him, "Son, go pick up
some kindling for the fire; go on out there and help Papa in
the field; the bucket is empty, walk on up there to the spring
and bring back some water."

Although as a child, not yet turned four, he had not learned
to read, there was much writing on the walls all about him,
for his mamma (we called her Anney), had covered them
with pages from newspapers and Sears Roebuck catalogs.

Not long thereafter, he realized how light a cotton sack
was early in the morning as he made his way to the cotton
field while the roosters crowed, and he learned how heavy
it could be as he pulled it back down the last of his rows
late in the evening.

He learned about churning milk, and milking cows, and

curing meat, and making fires in the old pot-bellied stoves, and trimming wicks to make lamp fires and cleaning lamp globes to make lamp fires brighter. And while he learned all this, late in the evening he learned, "Now I lay me down to sleep, I pray the Lord my soul to keep, If I should die before I wake, I pray the Lord my soul to take."

He learned to appreciate tea cakes, and shortening bread, and cracklins.

He learned that there actually was meat on chickens' feet and neck, and that hog head souse and hog jowls would make you just as full as a steak, if you were ever fortunate enough to get one.

Yes, home for this boy was Jefferson County where up on a hill, he heard the church folks at Mt. Israel singing-

> *Glory Glory Hallelujah*
> *Since I laid my burdens down*

He heard this singing as he made his way down the road with Anney, in their wagon bearing strictly lean and strictly fat candy to be shared with the other boys and girls after Sunday School and church that lasted well over five hours.

He went on to school where he learned to add, subtract, multiply and divide-

> *Add up his blessings-*
> *Subtract heartaches and pain,*
> *Multiply what God had given them*
> *And divide—for it is better to give, than to receive.*

He learned "Twinkle, twinkle, little star, how I wonder what you are"   *But* he also learned who made the stars twinkle.

He learned and knew well the value of a good education and recited, "He who knows not and knows that he knows not - is a child, teach him. He who knows and knows not that he knows—is asleep, awaken him. He who knows not and knows not that he knows not, is a fool, shun him. But he who knows and knows that he knows is a wise man, follow him."

He was so excited about learning and reciting until one

day his teacher assigned him a speech in the Easter Play -
the words went like this -

"Skipping down the shady lane, skipping down the dell"

And he became so excited, and skipped so hard and high
until he fell off the stage.

He got up and skipped on out the front door because he
felt surely the teacher was going to whip him for messing
up the program.

He learned early that he could not go through some doors,
not because of black mud on his feet, but because of the
blackness of his face. He stood and listened as his mother
and father were told that although they had worked their
hands to the bones, tilling, plowing the land, planting and
picking cotton, that they had come up short on their account at the general store. And he would return home with
them to get a little rest as the shadows of evening fell and
his mamma sang-

> *"I once was lost in sin, but Jesus took me in, and then
> a little light from heaven filled my soul- It filled my
> heart with love and wrote my name above and just a
> little with Jesus makes it right."*

Her little talks with Jesus may not have made everything
right, but somehow it made it bearable as she tucked him
into bed on a mattress stuffed with cotton and he rested his
little head on pillows cased in lily white sacks that formerly
had held flour.

Time passed and eventually the little boy was a teenager,
sharp, smart, alert, inquisitive, and yes, into those things
expected of boys his age.

His makeshift toys inclusive of bows and arrows, sling
shots and bolo bats somehow no longer held his attention.

Some years passed and his path crossed with that of a beautiful young lady named Rosa Lee Synder. Not long thereafter they found themselves standing before a preacher as they
promised to love and to cherish, in sickness and in health
for better or for worse until death they would part.

As a team, with both pulling hard together, realizing that
what God had joined together, no man should set asunder,

they continued to live by the sweat of their brows with him not wanting her behind him, but by his side.

In 1943 they decided to move from old man Waggoner's Plantation, but not without resistance. Jim was told that if he packed up to move, he would be killed. Nonetheless, he slipped away in the night, carrying his wife and six children.

Vicksburg was their destination. They found a shotgun house in Smith's Alley where he paid only $10 once for rent and immediately began to buy it.

Yes, they were still buying a house, but more than that, they had made a home—a home that was shared by everybody- a home where many lessons were taught— such as—

> *Put up a dry stick for a wet day, every road has to end somewhere, a house divided against itself cannot stand.*

These lessons were accompanied by music—music from the soul of James T. who went around humming -

> *Central's never busy,*
> *Always on the line,*
> *You can hear from Heaven almost any time-*
> *'Tis a royal service built for one and all-*
> *When you get in trouble, give this royal line a call.*

And from the loving heart of Rosa Lee who stirred in her pots as she sang—

> *Each day I'll do a golden deed*
> *To prove myself a friend in need-*
> *I'll labor on, until I die*
> *To reach my home up in the sky.*
>
> *To be a child of God each day,*
> *My light must shine along the way-*
> *I'll sing His praise as ages roll,*
> *And try to save somebody's soul.*

The songs continued right up the alley at Mt. Carmel Church where they had joined. Then later these songs were magnified by the notes of an old piano as the family would gather around and sing-

> *Time is filled with swift transition,*

Naught of earth unmoved can stand,
Build your hopes on things eternal,
Hold to God's unchanging hand.

The music never ceased as James T. and Rosa Lee opened a market in Marcus Bottom. James T. had also gone to work at Vicksburg Paint and Glass Company and some years later, another song was added to the list:

O' freedom, O' freedom,
O' freedom over me,
And before I be a slave,
I'll be buried in my grave
And go home to my Lord and be free.

James, Rosa and the children continued their quest for freedom, understanding quite well that, "Even the forces of a mighty army could not stop an idea whose time had come." (Victor Hugo)

And the years passed, the Chiplin family was blessed and increased many fold, adding daughters- and sons-in-law, grandchildren and great grand children.

In 1980, having lived and loved, cooked and served, wept with and prayed for so many people, Rosa had to leave.

James made a home for himself in Clinton, but he never forgot the love and fond memories of Vicksburg, Mississippi.

Yes, he did much to make everywhere—home—

- At Mt. Carmel where he struggled toe to toe to get the new building constructed and furnished.

- Here at Bethel A.M.E. Church, where he labored hard with his Masonic brothers and sisters to erect the statue of Thomas Stringer who founded masonry here in this very spot.

You see, he was not content as long as he knew somebody was hungry, it was then he fed them.

Somebody was without clothes, it was then, that he clothed them.

Somebody was sick, it was then that he visited them!

And the other day, he decided to head for another home—on

157

the wings of a dove.
Not an eagle—although it can cut the wind swiftly with its mighty wings and fly into yonders distance,

Not a mockingbird, although he fills the morning breeze with its song,-

But, on the wings of a dove, he went home-

Because the dove is peaceful, the dove is the Son of God.

> There's a land beyond the river
> That they call the sweet forever,
> And we only reach that shore by faith's decree-
> One by one, we'll cross the portal,
> There to dwell with the immortal,
> When they ring those golden bells
> for you and me....

Walking down from the pulpit with tears streaming down, I stopped at Daddy's coffin and said:

> My heart can sing when I pause to remember—

> A heartache here is but a stepping stone along a path,
> That's always winding upward;
> This troubled world is not my final home.

> These things of earth will dim and lose their value;
> But we recall, they're borrowed for a while;
> These things on earth that cause our hearts to tremble—
> Remember there, they will only bring a smile.

> But until then, my heart will go on singing;
> Until then, with joy I'll carry on;
> Until the day my eyes behold the city,
> Until the day God calls me home.

As we drove away from Bethel, the thunderous tolling of the bell was chilling to my spirit. It reminded me that in reality the bell was not tolling for our Daddy, but for us, the living—the living in fear of our own people!

After the State Masonic graveside ceremony, they lowered Daddy to his final resting place. As our limousine drove off, I looked back up the hill and I knew deep in my heart that there lies a black man who had been bound, but remained free. He had been bound by this nation's chains of racial discrimination and social injustice and hate directed towards the black cat. He had been and was now free—gone home on the wings of a dove.

THE END

"For Whom the Bell Tolls"—The bell tower of Bethel A.M.E. Church, Vicksburg, birthplace of Masonry in Mississippi and site of Mr. Chiplin's funeral.

ROADS

A CONSIDERATION OF THE ROADS FOR PRESENT DAY AMERICA, PARTICULARLY <u>YOUNG AMERICA</u>

The story of the Chiplin family is a story understood and shared by black families across the nation during our recent past. Many parents, married and single, used the basic components of Jim and Rosa Chiplin's child rearing and it worked. Parents and children of this time should at least consider the "roads" and give them a try.

FIRST ROAD—KNOW YOURSELF

As a beginning road from the Bottom, the process of knowing yourself is influenced by family and others around you who are familiar with your ancestry. Telling "who you are" should be accomplished without necessarily mentioning your name.

Many things make you who you are, including:

1. What your ethnic background is—what mixture of race, if any, are part of your biological inheritance
2. Who your parents, grandparents and other immediate relatives are
3. Your feelings, attitudes, ambitions, and the like further identify who you are ("As a man thinketh in his heart, so is he.")

Please be reminded constantly that who you are does not have to be dictated by where you are or the people around you. A rose in a bed of dandelions is still a rose. Refuse to be controlled by negative ennvironmental factors. Remember, "You do not have to move from the Bottom, to leave the Bottom."

SECOND ROAD— RESPECT FOR YOURSELF AND OTHERS

Far too many Americans have lost respect first for themselves and subsequently for others. We are judged in the eyes of others for the things we say and do. Moreover, we are judged in the eyes of God. Lose living, vulgar speech, vulgar dance, radios blasting rap profanity infect and infest our souls and being negatively.

Demand the respect of children and give them the same. Children: "Honor thy Father and Mother that thy days may be long upon the land which the Lord, thy God giveth." Parents should also remember the end of that scripture: "Fathers (mothers), provoke not thy children to wrath."

Your level of personal respect is reflected in a number of things:

1. Your personal appearance
2. What you say
3. What you do
4. Who you choose as your regular associates

No matter what color, if you trace your biological identity, there is much to be proud of. By all means, if you are black, your ancestral review reveals that you are the descendants of empire builders, great queens and kings, inventors, discoverers, great thinkers, and in most cases, slaves—not only of the American slave system, but past world slavery, including that of the children of Israel. As this is true, respect can also result from your refusal to be enslaved—to other people or things.

Aretha Franklin, in her recording—"Respect" said R-E-S-P-E-C-T, you know what it means to me—give it to me! Give it to me!..." As you give respect, in the classroom, on the job, at church, at home, all places, you will also be respected.

THIRD ROAD—FAITH

Access what you firmly believe to be true. Count on that, invest your every waking moment in that. Jessie Jackson instructs, "If the mind can conceive it and the heart can believe it, you can achieve it." Dare to "dream impossible dreams" and be willing to stand secure and watch them materialize. A nation without faith will not long endure.

So it is for a city, town, community or family, and individual. The very survival of blacks in slavery in America, blacks of the Reconstruction era and the Civil Rights era was linked to faith—faith to believe a better day would come, as would strength enough to see to it that it did.

"Where there is no faith in the future—there is no power in the present." Condition your mind to think progressive thoughts. Take a look at what is and envision what it can become. ("For if ye have faith the size of a grain of mustard seed, you can say to the mountains—be thou moved."

FOURTH ROAD—A GOOD EDUCATION

We have been instructed in the Bible to *"study"* to show thyself approved, a workman who needs not be ashamed." The human mind is fascinating and has unlimited potential and power. Borrowing from the United Negro College Fund, "A mind is a terrible thing to waste." Consider what you think about. Make sure your thoughts are positive. Thoughts lead to actions; actions to habits; habits to character and character to our final destiny.

Perhaps you may have dropped out of school for various reasons. Don't let that stop you from learning. The world is your classroom—there is so much to learn. If practical, you can seek assistance and study for your General Education Development GED exam— and pass it!!

Mary McLeod Bethune, one of America's most highly respected and articulate educators of the past, was often teased about her dark skin and called, "old black gal." She defended herself only by saying, "They say I am black as midnight, but I stay up later than midnight and I learn." Books left in school lockers, assignments not done, attention not paid in class will certainly result in any student's failure. The streets are filled with people who failed to try, people who have greater chances of getting killed.

FIFTH ROAD—NEVER GIVE UP!

So often we heard as children, "If at first you don't succeed, try, try, again." It works. Works in the classroom, on

163

the job, at home, in the church, and yes, in romantic relations. Be determined not to lose no matter how difficult life gets. Patience and endurance are priceless commodities. ("When life seems rough as it sometimes will; when the road you are traveling seems all uphill; when care is pressing you down a bit—rest if you must, but don't you quit!"

We can gain courage from the little weak boy in Daddy's story of the "Mountain Climber" on page 38. Although thought to be a weakling, with strong determination he made it to the top of the mountain. As climbers of life's mountain, it is easy to become discouraged by criticism, negative specualtion, and constant reminders of our limitations. Keep your head lifted up, look towards the mountain top, keep climbing, although at times you may lose your foothold and slip. Remember, "The deeper the valley, the higher the mountain top; the greater the challenge, the better the victory; the darker the night, the greater the appreciation of the day."

SIXTH ROAD—ASSOCIATE WITH PEOPLE WHO ARE TRYING TO ADVANCE

It is impossible to "hitch your wagon to a star" that's on the ground. If we are to move ahead in our lives, not only must our aims be high, but we must hang out with others who also have high aims. A present blues tune shares, "I can do bad all by myself, I don't need nobody else to help me do bad!" Yes, it's true that "Misery loves company." Do not allow anybody to pull you down, suppress your dreams, or make you feel little.

Above all, remember that looking up to people who make fast money illegally will get you in trouble. Most drug dealers have been to jail or are on the way. In my assignment as program coordinator and rehabilitation counselor for the Hinds County Sheriff's Department, I have seen far too many young men whose associations with the wrong people have brought them excessively long jail and prison sentences. Never think that you are smart enough not to get caught. That's dumb!!

SEVENTH ROAD—HELP SOMEBODY ELSE

One of the lessons we were taught as children was about "crabs in a barrel." My father pointed out that you don't have to put a top on a barrel of crabs. Each time one has almost made it to the top, another reaches up and pulls him back down. The crab lesson can be applied to our human efforts to advance. As we reach out to help others, we are helped.

St. Francis of Assisi suggested that "It is in giving that we receive, and in dying that we are born to eternal life." A basic equation of life is, "Give equals get." The more we are willing to give of our time, assistance, understanding, love and material gain, the more of the same we receive. It turns out that life is like a boomerang—whatever we throw in the distance returns to us.

In the movie "Lean On Me", the theme song reminds us..."You just call on me, brother, if you need a hand; we all need somebody to lean on; you just might have a problem that I understand; we all need somebody to lean on."

EIGHTH ROAD—STAND UP FOR SOMETHING

Martin L. King often said, "The man who has not found something worth giving his life for is not fit to live." Mrs. Ruby Triplett, one of my seventh grade teachers, shared a poem with us, "I fight a battle every day against discouragement and fear; some foe is always in my way; the path ahead is never clear—I struggle as I press along, but fighting keeps my spirit strong." (author unknown)

In the "Vernon Johns Story" recently aired on T.V., Vernon Johns, who preceded Martin L. King as pastor of Dexter Avenue Baptist Church in Montgomery, Alabama said, "If you see a good fight—get in it!" His reference was to the fight for human dignity. There are so many worthy causes that need our assistance—our fighting spirits. It is certainly true that, "If you don't stand for something, you will fall for anything."

NINTH ROAD—TRUST IN GOD

It is so unfortunate that many black people today have disassociated themselves with church and even claim not to believe in God. Some of them say that "The white man wrote the Bible." That statement itself is historically incorrect—and how do you know that? I am sure that many black people have searched for excuses to keep them from living Christian lives. To dismiss God gives the individual more freedom to live a reckless life. While there may be much wrong in many churches, there is still a lot of good to be found there. Coming together (assembling ourselves together as believers), whether it is at the church, temple, or tent, helps to reinforce our beliefs and provides fellowship that we so desperately need. Trust in God no matter who sins, no matter who is hypocritical, no matter who does not.

TENTH ROAD—PRAY

Each of the previously mentioned roads is enhanced through our prayers. The reverent act of kneeling spiritually and physically denotes our respect for and belief in a higher being—somebody bigger than ourselves. To some His name is God, to others Jehovah; many call Him Allah, Messiah, Yahweh, or another name. It is most important that we know and call Him something, ask for His guidance and strength and firmly believe that He will hear and answer our prayers. Remember: "He who spends sufficient time on his knees will have no trouble standing on his feet."

ROSES FOR ROSE

Has been a while since you went away
Up in heaven with Jesus to stay,
Yet we remember, we love you still
As years roll past, we always will.

And now the roses remain in our heart
The beautiful roses, will never depart
For they remind us of your spirit and love
So rest on dear Rose, with Jesus above.

The lives you have touched, the joy that you gave
The many small children you tried to save
Bring memories of roses when we think of you
The loveliest of roses, tender and true.

Jessie and Johnnie, Edward and James
Think of the roses when we call your name
T. J. and Buddy have memories fond.
Of one sweet Rose, who has gone beyond.

And one day we'll meet you when the roses will fade
For Jesus our Savior, the debt has paid—
So rest on awhile, until we meet,
And cast our roses at the Master's feet.

POETRY AND INSPIRATION
From The Bottom of My Heart
by Charles Kinnard Chiplin

TIMES AND THINGS I REMEMBER

The times that I remember, the times gone by we had -
Back down in Marcus Bottom, with Momma and with Dad.
Even now I smell the market, where they sold all kinds of
    fish,
Let me go back for a moment, to fulfill my greatest wish.
With Jessie Lee and Johnnie, Edward Lee and Boo too,
Playing up and down the alley, with Janice Lee and Lou.
All the moments I remember somehow now still touch my
    heart,
All the good times and the bad times, came and left, we had
    to part.
Boo was bad, and killed the chickens, Mr. D. C. had a fit!
Came out shouting "Boo, what happened?!" He replied, "I
    deadened it!"
Buddy and T. J. were in service and were often gone away,
Served our country in the army, as did our brother Ray.
Sunday dinner on the table, Momma cooked and fed us all,
Homemade rolls and fried chicken, these are things I recall.

I recall the great tornado back in 1953, just a few days be-
    fore Christmas
When the limbs fell out the tree.
Daddy worked as a glazier, climbing ladders, cutting glass.
I remember "Jim's Glass Ship," just a few things from the
    past.
Not much money, fame or fortune, just good folks with
    hearts of love.
Struggling, toiling, helping, hoping, as we served the man
    above.
I remember the old piano where we often gathered 'round.
"Golden Bells" and "Rock of Ages," hymns of glory would
    resound.

I remember cutting neckbones in the former "WaJu Store;"
Slicing bacon, pumping coal oil, sweeping dust up from the
floor.
Then there came the awful bombing back in 1965, in No-
vember, on fourth Sunday,
It is luck we're alive!
Didn't stop us, we worked harder; Daddy never closed the
door,
But, he went on selling hamhocks, I remember that and
more.

Bags and buckets from the college where Momma was em-
ployed,
No we never can forget her, all her children she enjoyed.
Though sometimes we tried her patience, she was there to
hear our cry.
Now, she's left us, and we miss her, but we know the rea-
son why.
For somewhere up in glory, 'round the throne, I know she's
there.
Probably cooking for the Savior, as she hums "Sweet Hour
of Prayer."
Yes, the things that I remember, never can you take away,
For I've stored them up forever, and they brighten up my
day.
I can smile when I remember riding in the truck to Fayette
Or when spending nights with Aney, sleeping in the old iron
bed.
Uncle Andrew, and Aunt Shirley, Corrie Lee, the children
too,
Ollie Bell and Uncle Edward, these are names I share with
you.
For so vivid in my memory are the people we hold dear,
And they made our lives worth living, in our hearts we'll
keep them near.

ODE TO ROSA LEE

(Dedicated to: Jessie, Boo, Johnnie, T. J., Buddy, Edward Lee, Daddy and all the rest of her folks, grandchildren, greatgrandchildren, former daughters-in-law, present daughters-in-law, her mother, sister and brother)

She gleaned in the fields till sunset
Her hours of struggle long —
Rosa kept right on working,
Her life expressed her song.
Met James back in the country,
where cotton and potatoes grew;
They traveled the road together,
Rekindled their love anew.
James and Rosa and the children,
Decided to move to town —
Leaving behind their kindred,
A house in the alley found.
Cooking was her profession,
She was the very best —
She worked and raised the children,
With taking little rest.
Religion was her refuge;
The Bible was her guide;
It helped to see her over,
Her husband by her side.
A strong and able woman,
Though black, her face was light—
She held on to her honor,
And treated everybody right.
Up early in the morning,
Cooking and getting things done—
And toiling to the midday
And to the setting sun.
Having borne nine little black children,
And two of them had died,
Rosa had no time for stopping,
Sometimes at evening cried.
Beauty filled each passing hour,

171

Through grace the moments rolled;
Wisdom was her virtue,
And patience filled her soul.
But came the days of conflict,
With trials to press, confound —
She never once relented;
Though her spirit was cast down.
The years of work and business,
At the former WaJu Store,
She handled like a hero,
Did all of this and more.
She fed the freedom workers,
And saved a life or two,
Nothing was too valued,
For her to give to you.

A BLACK MOTHER

(A tribute to the memory of my mother, the late Rosa L. Chiplin)

Pressed by the years, beset with tears,
Struggling to make ends meet
With blisters on her feet—a Black Mother.
Wondering when the day
She would get her pay
And hear her children say—She's my mother.
All through the long night hours,
Her tears came down like showers,
But her blessings bloom like flowers—a Black Mother.
She bears the pains of labor,
Yet never does she waver:
Her children she does savor—She's their mother.
With debts that must be paid,
She can't sit in the shade:
She calls a spade a spade—She's some mother!
And oft misunderstood,
And no one sees her good:
She's done the best she could—a Black Mother.
She stands up to the foes.
And struggles as she goes:
Her anguish really shows—a tired mother.
Almost too weak to moan,
The children now are grown—a Black Mother.
Yet through the bitter cold,
Her footsteps are untold,
Although she's growing old—a Black Mother.
She sees her sons depart,
As sorrow fills her heart —
For she gave them their start—the lonely mother.
Her daughters too must leave,
Their husbands to receive,
And no one will believe—she's their mother.
She often kneels to pray,
Her hair has now turned gray:
And you can hear her say—I'm their mother.
The house is now run down,

Little joy there to be found
Few people come around—to see mother.
Dear God, in heaven on high,
Look down and hear me cry,
And show the reason why—a Black Mother
Who gave the best she had,
Now sits alone and sad —
Please make her poor heart glad—a Black Mother.
And soon she'll get her wings,
As the choir of angels sings,
And the bells of heaven ring—She's still mother.
And at the setting of the sun,
When our work on earth is done,
And the victory is won—we'll see Mother!

BLACK FATHER TO SON

(A tribute to my father, James T. Chiplin, Sr.)

Now son, I gotta tell you,
Life for me done been one long, hard stair —
On my way to find the end of my rainbow.
But rainbows for black men ain't got no end son,
Just a beginning and a poorly lit
Sometimes dark, rock road
Where you stumble beneath the load,
Then yo' shoes gits tacks in 'em
That hurt and blister
And some folks don't understand,
Cause some folks ain't never wore them shoes
Some folks won't never feel yo' blues.
And you goes in places where the sign say WELCOME
But you knows you ain't wanted
By the silent stares and coldness in the place,
Not cause you a Christian,
But the color of yo' face.
Yet son, you goes on a-climbing
And a-reaching, hoping someday, somewhere
Long the rugged path
There be a ray of light —
But all you see is dark as night.
And you loves and no one believe you
Don't really understand —
That you have a heart, and you ache deep within
And you feel pain and joy
But they don't call you a man, just BOY.
And you dreams, but they don't come true,
Just disappear to somewhere out yonder.
You prays prayers that don't seem to be no answers for
And you feels a little behinder.
Then you sows yo' seeds son, hoping for a big crop—
You comes back later to gather your own —
Someone else got it and gone.
But you must go on a-dreaming and a-praying yo' prayers,
Keep on til yo' work is done,

For I knows that tomorrow you be a man,
And you gon have a son— And you be sure to tell him
Like Daddy told you today —
Rainbows for Black men just end that way.

WHY BLACK FOLKS SHOUT!

Trials and tribulation on every hand —
Risin' and falling, doing the best they can—
Is there any wonder—Is there any doubt —
With so many heartaches—why black folks shout!

Told to stand back, you're second class —
Hoping that freedom would come at last —
There is no wonder—there is no doubt —
With burdens on their backs—why black folks shout!

Blisters on their feet,—blisters in their hands —
Digging and a' toting—trying to plow the land —
Did you ever wonder, did you ever doubt —
Treated like a packhorse—why black folks shout!

Days of segregation—and days of old Jim Crow,
Sent out in the kitchen, his black face not to show —
Should you ever wonder, should you ever doubt —
With all the odds against him—why black folks shout!

But came the Sunday morning—he would sing and pray
To his sweet Jesus, is there any doubt? —
Knowing the Lord would help him—why black folks shout!

THE ORGAN BUILDER

Day by day the organ builder sat alone in his chamber
　wrought —
As he fitted the parts together for the greatest organ—As he
　thought...
"This will be the greatest organ that the world has ever
　known" —
And daily he went on working, struggling, toiling all alone.
The people thought him crazy that he worked with so much
　care —
But he smiled and kept on working, softly humming, offer-
　ing prayer —
No, he didn't let it stop him—their stares and ridicule —
It didn't see to bother him—That they said he was a FOOL.
Great and massive was its structure—From the pedals to
　the top —
With great patience he placed the ivory—mastered each and
　every stop.
Yes, it really was some organ—Built with patience and much
　thought —
And it really pleased its maker—For perfection he had
　sought.
Just a day before completion—Of his greatest life's desire —
Tragedy struck, and left him weeping—For his home was
　swept with fire.
In his grief the builder cried out —
"Tell me now, what shall I do? I have done my best and
　struggled —
And it burned when I was through!"
Somehow though, he found the courage—to start his work
　anew —
Plundering through the ash and rubble—doing what he had
　to do.
Years again he went on working—He replaced each single
　part
With desire and dedication—driving ever in his heart.
At last, his job finished—He had given and suffered much

And the grand old organ builder—Gave his organ to the church.

Once again they called him crazy, Talked about him over town —
In his heart he found contentment, For his soul was heaven bound —
And then came next Sunday morning—All the bells rang out it's said —
For the grand old organ builder—Lay in the church yard—dead.
Yes—we all are organ builders—Or it seems that way to me —
We are fitting keys together that must play through eternity.

Black and white keys on the keyboard —
Make a melody of love —
That will last throughout the ages —
And will please our God above!

THE KEY TO ETERNITY
(Dedicated to Jessie and Johnnie)

Standing by the wayside with a stick in his hands —
There stood a way worn traveler, cast away from man.
His clothes were torn and tattered
His shoes a sight to see;
And in one of his age old hands—He held a sparkling key.
The children all engrossed in play, looked at the old man
As to say "He's to be pitied—He's out of his mind —
You find folks like him from time to time."

One, two, three hours passed by the old man
And not a single traveler lifted a helping hand.
Then, looking down the road, he spied a young comrade —
And from the expression on his face—he was then made
  glad.
The lad took him by the hands and led him down the road

He took him to his humble home—And lifted his heavy load.
He fed him and gave him clothes—he helped him, as you
  see —
And o'er the days the man would not let go
Of his shining, sparkling key.

Over a month had passed—he started doing fine —
He said to the young comrade—you will be made divine.
He whispered a word of prayer, and a verse of a song did
  sing —
And through the silence of the night—Bells began to ring.
Bells that rang out loud and clear to the men who passed
  him by —
Bells that sounded a doleful tune—to make us wonder why

We have no time to help and give another on the way.
So busy with our daily lives—Forgetting the prayers we pray

For daily bread, and food and clothes;
Forgiveness for another.
We close our hearts—Lock tight the doors —
Forgetting our starving brother.

He placed the key in the young man's hand and said —
"Forever be! For now, kind friend,
You have received THE KEY TO ETERNITY!"

"A Resting Place"—Grave of James T. and Rosa Lee Chiplin, Vicksburg City Cemetery.

CONCLUSION OF THE MATTER
Charles Kinnard Chiplin

It's a long road from the bottom
If you try to walk alone—
Your steps may be too feeble,
Seems sometimes your hope is gone.

You can make it from the bottom —-
Have respect for yourself and others;
Remembering who helped you make it
Not forgetting less fortunate brothers.

Though your body may never move,
And remain bound by a bottom space —
You can lift your aspirations,
Send your mind to a higher place.

The top is never crowded,
Lazy men and women stand
In places where without effort,
They can hang out in the land.

Choose a point that's high above you,
Chart your course, and make a start
You will make it from the bottom —
First believe it in your heart.

When by chance on higher plateaus,
Your weary feet arrive —
Don't forget who kept you going
And who will help you survive.

His name is Christ, Our Refuge,
The way, the Truth, the Light—
He will help you from the bottom —
Just look up,
He is in sight.

ABOUT THE AUTHOR

Charles Chiplin, born the last of eight children to Rosa Lee and James T. Chiplin, Sr., grew up in Vicksburg, Mississippi where his creative abilities were crystallized at an early age.

As a student in the public schools of Vicksburg, he was often called upon to write poems, plays and stories. Writing became an intricate part of his life as well as playing the piano and organ —gifts he realized at age eight.

He continued his education at Alcorn State University where he earned the Bachelor of Science Degree in Sociology in 1970. In 1973 he received the Master of Arts Degree in Social Studies from Jackson State University and later attended Northeast Louisiana State University (1976-78) where he studied toward the Doctorate in Educational Administration and Supervision. His additional studies include—Tougaloo College, Louisiana State University, Arizona State University, South Carolina State University, the Mississippi Baptist Seminary and Mississippi College.

In 1970 he accepted the call to the ministry and served as an associate minister of Mt. Carmel M. B. Church in Vicksburg. His religious experiences include serving as past minister of music and organist of Greater Mt. Calvary Baptist Church, Jackson, Mississippi and present Associate Minister and Organist of Cade Chapel M. B. Church, Jackson, Mississippi.

He is employed as an instructor at Yazoo City High School, Yazoo City, Mississippi, where he teaches government and black history. Additionally, he is a deputy with the Hinds County Sheriff's Department and serves as program coordinator. Charles has written 40 stage plays, seven screenplays, and scores of poems and short stories.

He sums up his life's motto simply by saying, *"If I can help somebody as I pass along, then my living shall not be in vain."*